if your local library does not hold a particular book, the librarian should be able to tell you where to find it — and, as a last resort, may be able to borrow it for you via the inter-library loan network, irrespective of whether you live in London or San Francisco. Many overseas libraries have good collections of books on English genealogy and local history, for example, several of the Australian state libraries. The libraries of family history societies are also worth checking — even if they are far distant from Yorkshire: for example, the Genealogical Society of Victoria, in Melbourne, has a good collection of books on English genealogy. Some family history societies offer a postal borrowing service; others may be willing to check a particular book for you. It is also worth joining one of the genealogical newsgroups or mailing lists on the internet; other members may hold the books you need, and be willing to check them for you.

In general, I have not included works which are national in scope but which have local content. Many such works may be identified in *English genealogy: a bibliography,* to which reference is made at appropriate points below. The innumerable notes and queries to be found in family history society journals etc., are excluded, except where their content is of importance. Where I have included such notes, replies to them are cited in the form 'see also', with no reference to the names of respondents. I have also excluded extracts from newspapers, and histories which have not been published. Where possible, citations are accompanied by notes indicating the period covered, the locality/ies concerned, and other pertinent information. Most of the items listed here have been physically examined to ensure that they are relevant, and that correct bibliographical details are given. However, a few items have proved elusive, and yet worthy of mention; these are noted 'not seen', and I cannot guarantee the accuracy of the information provided in these entries.

For Yorkshire, so much information has been published that no less than 6 volumes are required to list relevant citations. This volume identifies innumerable works relating to the administration of government - national, county, and local - the church, and private estates. Such works contain an enormous mass of information of importance for genealogists, and may enable many links to be made. Indeed, there is too much information for one volume to contain; consequently, a number of sources emanating from administrative action are treated in other volumes of *Yorkshire: the genealogists library guide,* e.g. parish registers and probate records in volume

5

2, and official lists of names in volume 3. This volume concentrates on those sources created in the process of administration, although related topics are also considered.

Four further volumes of *Yorkshire: the genealogists library guide* list the wide range of published sources that are available; the final volume lists innumerable published family histories and pedigrees. All of these volumes may also include information relevant to the contents of this volume, which is not repeated here.

Be warned: just because information has been published, it does not necessarily follow that it is accurate. I have not made any judgement on the accuracy of most works listed: that is up to you.

If you are an assiduous researcher, you may well come across items I have missed. If you do, please let me know, so that they can be included in the next edition.

The work of compiling this bibliography has depended heavily on the resources of the libraries I have used. These included the local studies collections in the public libraries of Bradford, Doncaster, Hull, Leeds, Sheffield, and York, the Brotherton Library at the University of Leeds, the British Library, the Society of Genealogists, Guildhall Library, the University and the Central Library in Bristol, the University of Exeter library and the Exeter Public Library in Exeter. I have also used the resources of a number of family history societies, and am particularly grateful to the societies for Devon, Cornwall, Somerset & Dorset, Sheffield and Ripon/Harrogate. All these institutions deserve my thanks, as does John Perkins, who read and commented on an early draft of the book. Cynthia Hanson and Paul Raymond typed the manuscript, and Bob Boyd saw the book through the press. I am grateful too to the officers of the Federation of Family History Societies, whose support is vital for the continuation of this series. My thanks also to my wife Marjorie.

Stuart A. Raymond

Contents

Front cover: Monk Bar with portcullis down

Introduction

This guide to published sources of genealogical information is intended primarily for genealogists. It is, however, hoped that it will also prove useful to historians, librarians, archivists, research students, and anyone else interested in the history of Yorkshire. It is intended to be used in conjunction with my *English genealogy: a bibliography,* with the other volumes of *Yorkshire: the genealogists library guide,* and with the companion volumes in the *British genealogical library guides* series. A full list of these volumes appears on the back cover.

Many genealogists, when they begin their research, do not realise just how much information has been published, and is readily available in printed form. Not infrequently, they head straight for the archives, rather than checking printed sources first. In so doing, they waste much time, and also impose needless wear and tear on irreplaceable archives. However, when faced with the vast array of tomes possessed by major reference libraries, it is difficult to know where to begin without guidance. This bibliography is intended to point you in the right direction. My aim has been to list everything relating to Yorkshire that has been published and is likely to be of use to genealogists. However, anyone who tries to compile a totally comprehensive bibliography of Yorkshire is likely to fall short of his aim. The task is almost impossible, especially if the endeavour is made by one person. That does not, however, mean that the attempt should not be made. Usefulness, rather than comprehensiveness, has been my prime aim - and this book would not be useful to anyone if its publication were to be prevented by a vain attempt to ensure total comprehensiveness. I am well aware that there are likely to be omissions, especially in view of the fact that, given constraints of time and money, it has not been possible for me to visit all of the large number of libraries with substantial collections on Yorkshire's history. Each of them may well possess works not held anywhere else. The identification of such works is not, however, a major aim of this bibliography. Rather, my purpose has been to enable you to identify works which are mostly readily available. Some titles you may be able to purchase; all can be found in libraries throughout the English-speaking world. You can check the holdings of many libraries via their catalogues on the internet; alternatively,

Abbreviations

B.A.	*Bradford Antiquary*
B.I.B.	*Borthwick Institute bulletin*
B.S.H.S.	*Bulletin of the Saddleworth Historical Society*
B.T.C.	Borthwick texts and calendars: records of the Northern Provinces.
Bk.I.H.R	*Borthwick Institute of Historical Research*
B.T.	*Banyan tree: journal of the East Yorkshire Family History Society*
C.R.S.	*Catholic Record Society*
C.T.L.H.S.B.	*Cleveland and Teeside Local History Society bulletin*
C.Y.D.F.H.S.N.	*City of York & District Family History Society newsletter*
Cameo	*Cameo: Morley & District Family History Group newsletter*
Don. Anc.	*Doncaster ancestor*
E.Y.L.H.S.	East Yorkshire Local History Society series
F.H.S.	Family History Society
F.S.	*The flowing stream: journal of the Sheffield and District Family History Society*
H. & D F.H.S.J.	*Huddersfield & District Family History Society journal*
J.Cl.F.H.S.	*Journal of the Cleveland Family History Society*
K.D.F.H.S.J.	*Keighley & District Family History and Heraldry Society journal*
N.H.	*Northern history*
N.Y.C.R.O.P.	North Yorkshire County Record Office publications
O.W.R.	*Old West Riding*
P.R.H.A.S.	*Papers, reports, etc., read before the Halfax Antiquarian Society*
R. & D.F.H.S.N.	*Rotherham and District Family History Society newsletter*
R.H.	*Ripon historian*

T.E.R.A.S.	*Transactions of the East Riding Archaeological Society*
T. Hal. A.S.	*Transactions of the Halifax Archaeological Society*
T. Hunter A.S.	*Transactions of the Hunter Archaeological Society*
T.R.S.	*Teesdale Record Society [proceedings]*
T.S.	Thoresby Society
Wh.N.	*Wharfedale newsletter: the journal of the Wharfedale Family History Group*
Y.A.J.	*Yorkshire Archaeolgical Society*
Y.A.S., F.H.P.S.S.N.	*Yorkshire Archaeological Society. Family History and Population Studies Section Newsletter*
Y.A.S., R.S.	Yorkshire Archaeological Society. Record Series
Y.A.S., W.C.R.S.	Yorkshire Archaeological Society. Wakefield Court Rolls series
Y.C.M.	*Yorkshire county magazine*
Y.F.H.	*Yorkshire family historian*
Y.F.H.S.N.	*York Family History Society newsletter*
Y.G.	*Yorkshire genealogist*
Y.N.Q. I.	*Yorkshire notes & queries* [1888-90]
Y.N.Q. II.	*Yorkshire notes & queries* [1905-9]

Bibliographic Presentation

Authors names are in SMALL CAPITALS. Book and journal titles are in *italics*. Articles appearing in journals, and material such as parish register transcripts, forming only part of books are in inverted commas and textface type. Volume numbers are in **bold** and the individual number of the journal may be shown in parentheses. These are normally followed by the place of publication (except where this is London, which is omitted), the name of the publisher and the date of publication. In the case of articles, further figures indicate page numbers.

Libraries and Record Offices

Many libraries have substantial collections of books and journals on Yorkshire history; only a select list of addresses can be given here. I have not included the addresses of most family history societies, whose libraries are available to their members, and which ought to be used by everyone tracing their ancestors in the area covered. Their addresses change frequently, and any listing would be out of date by the time it was printed. Current addresses are regularly published in *Family history news & digest.*

I have also excluded the addresses of most Yorkshire record repositories. These hold the archives you may need to consult, but generally speaking do not have large collections of printed books.

It is also worth pointing out that many public and university libraries throughout the English-speaking world hold much Yorkshire material; in particular, many university libraries subscribe to major series such as the *Yorkshire archaeological journal* and the Yorkshire Archaeological Society's *Record series* - which may also be available in the libraries of the major county historical societies who exchange journals with them.

Major collections of Yorkshire material are to be found in at least two London institutions:

British Library
96, Euston Road,
London,
NW1 2DB

Society of Genealogists,
14, Charterhouse Buildings,
Goswell Road,
London,
EC1M 7BA

The two Yorkshire institutions with a county-wide remit are:

Borthwick Institute,
University of York,
St.Anthony's Hall
Peasholme Green,
York, YO1 2PW

Yorkshire Archaeological Society
Claremont,
23, Clarendon Road,
Leeds,
LS2 9NZ

A number of university libraries in the county have important Yorkshire collections:

Brynmor Jones Library,
University of Hull,
Hull, HU6 7RX
(Houses the East Yorkshire Bibliography)

Brotherton Library
University of Leeds
Leeds, LS2 9JT

The major local collections in public libraries are:

Bradford
Bradford Central Library
Princes Way,
Bradford,
BD1 1NN

Hull
Local Studies Library,
Hull Central Library
Albion Street,
Hull, HU1 3TF

Leeds
Local History Collection,
Central Library,
Calverley Street,
Leeds, LS1 3AB

Middlesbrough
Local Collection,
Middlesbrough Reference Library,
Victoria Square,
Middlesbrough,
Cleveland,
TS1 2AY

Sheffield
Local Studies Library,
Sheffield City Libraries,
Surrey Street,
Sheffield, S1 1XZ

York
York City Library,
Reference Library,
Local Studies Collection,
Museum Street,
York, YO1 2DS

1. RECORDS OF NATIONAL AND COUNTY GOVERNMENT

Government bureaucracy is responsible for many of the sources used by genealogists. Many publications based on these sources are listed in other parts of this bibliography, e.g. vol.3, *Yorkshire lists of names.* Here, the intention is to identify those works which list officials, e.g. Members of Parliament, or which calendar sources such as Quarter Sessions records. Sources such as these record innumerable people inter-acting with government in a variety of ways, all of which may have genealogical interest.

A. *Members of Parliament*

The authoritative guide to Yorkshire Members of Parliament is now:

GOODER, A., ed. *The Parliamentary representation of the County of York, 1258-1832.* 2 vols. Y.A.S., R.S. **91 & 96.** 1935-8.

A number of other works are also available:

BEAN, WILLIAM WARDELL. *The Parliamentary representation of the six northern counties of England: Cumberland, Durham, Lancashire, Northumberland, Westmoreland and Yorkshire, and their cities and boroughs, from 1603 to the general election of 1886, with lists of members and biographical notices.* Hull: Charles Henry Barnwell, 1890.

PARK, GODFREY RICHARD. *The Parliamentary representation of Yorkshire from the earliest representative Parliament on record in the reign of King Edward I to the dissolution of the twenty-second Parliament in the reign of Queen Victoria.* Hull: Charles Henry Barnwell, 1886.

SMITH, HENRY STOOKS. *The Parliamentary representation of Yorkshire.* John Russell Smith, 1854. Lists M.Ps for the county.

TAYLOR, R.V. 'Yorkshire M.Ps', *Y.G.* **1,** 1888, *passim.* Biographical dictionary.

TAYLOR, R.V. 'Old Yorkshire M.Ps', *Y.G.* **1,** 1888, *passim.*

TAYLOR, R.V. 'Old Yorkshire M.Ps', *Y.C.M.* **3,** 1893, 133-46.

'Yorkshire M.Ps in 1753', *Y.N.Q.I.* **1,** 1888, 5-6. Brief list.

MARKHAM, JOHN. *Nineteenth-century Parliamentary elections in East Yorkshire.* E.Y.L.H.S. **37.** 1982. Includes list of candidates.

Aldborough and Boroughbridge

LAWSON-TANCRED, THOMAS, SIR. 'Parliamentary history of Aldborough and Boroughbridge', *Y.A.J.* **27,** 1924, 325-62. Includes notes on M.Ps.

Halifax

'Yorkshire Parliamentary representatives: Halifax Parliamentary representation', *Old Yorkshire* **5,** 1894, 286-8. List of M.Ps for Halifax, 1832-82.

York

EBOR. 'Members of Parliament for York, 1713-1832', *Y.N.Q.I.* **1,** 1888, 20-23. List with brief notes.

SHIELDS, ELIZABETH L. 'The members of Parliament for the city of York, 1485-1515', *York historian* **11,** 1994, 9-21. Includes list of 16 M.Ps.

B. *Sheriffs and Lords Lieutenants*

FARRER, W. 'Sheriffs of Lincolnshire and Yorkshire, 1066-1130', *English historical review* **30,** 1915, 277-85. Traces holders of the office.

PACKETT, C. NEVILLE. *The West Yorkshire lieutenancy: list of Lord-Lieutenants, 1547-1978.* Bradford: the author, 1978.

C. *Medieval Records*

A variety of medieval records, e.g. pipe rolls, recording the sources of the Kings' income, and records of eyres, i.e. courts of law, are available in print; these mention many names, and are listed here in rough chronological order.

'Yorkshire records', *Y.A.J.* **3,** 1875, 392-403. Yorkshire extracts from the pipe roll, 1131-2, and from the *Red book of the Exchequer* late 12th c.

CLAY, CHARLES TRAVIS, ed. *Three Yorkshire assize rolls for the reigns of King John and King Henry III.* Y.A.S., R.S. **44.** 1911.

'Assize roll 1039. Pleas heard at York and elsewhere before the King, the Justiciar, and other judges', in STENTON, DORIS MARY, ed. *Pleas before the King or his justices, volume III. Rolls or fragments of rolls from the years 1199, 1201, and 1203-6.* Selden Society **83**, 1966, 125-75. For 1204.

'Assize roll 1039. Pleas of the Crown at York, 1208', in STENTON, DORIS MARY, ed. *Pleas before the King or his justices, 1198-1212. Volume IV. Rolls or fragments of rolls from the years 1207-1212.* Selden Society **84**, 1967, 94-117.

STENTON, D.M., ed. *Rolls of justices in eyre, being the rolls of pleas and assizes for Yorkshire in 3 Henry III (1218-19).* Selden Society **56**. 1937.

ENGLISH, B.A. 'Additional records of the Yorkshire Eyre of 1218-19', *Y.A.J.* **48**, 1976, 95-6. Brief note.

LANCASTER, W.T., ed. 'Extracts from a Yorkshire assize roll, 3 Henry III, 1219', in *Miscellanea* **1**. Y.A.S., R.S. **61**. 1920, 170-85.

ENGLISH, BARBARA, ed. *Yorkshire hundred and quo warranto rolls.* Y.A.S., R.S. **151**. 1996. Late 13th c.

JEWELL, HELEN M. 'Local administration and administrators in Yorkshire, 1258-1348', *N.H.* **16**, 1980, 1-19.

KAYE, WALTER J. 'Yorkshiremen who declined to take up their knighthood, 1 Ric.II (1377) and 16 & 19 Hen.VII (1500 & 1503)', *Y.A.J.* **31**, 1934, 360-65. List.

'Yorkshire deodands', *Y.A.J.* **15**, 1898-9, 199-210. Transcript of a return of deodands. A deodand is 'that instrument which occasions the death of a man'.

C. *16-19th Century Records*

Yorkshire Star Chamber proceedings. Y.A.S., R.S. **41, 45, 51 & 70**. 1909-27. *Temp.* Henry VII and Henry VIII.

BROOKS, F.W. *York and the Council of the North.* St. Anthony's Hall Publications **5**. St. Anthony's Press, 1954.

ROBINSON, ALAN. 'The rising in the North', *C.Y.D.F.H.S.N.* **39**, 1996, 6-7. Includes list of rebels executed in Richmondshire, after the 1569 rebellion.

'Pardons', *R.H.* **2**(8), 1994, 183-6. List of pardons granted following the rising of the northern earls, 1569.

BROOKS, F.W. *Yorkshire and the Star Chamber.* E.Y.L.H.S. **4**. 1954.

BREWSTER, NICHOLAS. 'Parties from Yorkshire in the list of schedules to the mayor's court original bills', *Y.F.H.* **16**(1), 8-9. Lists litigants in the Lord Mayor of London's court, 16-17th c.

[RAINE, JAMES, junior,] ed. *Depositions from the Castle of York relating to offences committed in the northern counties in the seventeenth century.* Surtees Society **40**. 1861.

BAILDON, W. PALEY. 'Compositions for not taking knighthoods at the coronation of Charles I', in *Miscellanea* **1**. Y.A.S., R.S. **61**, 1920, 84-107.

PEACOCK, EDWARD. 'On some Civil War documents relating to Yorkshire', *Y.A.J.* **1**, 1870, 89-106. Includes list of Royalist commanders, of prisoners taken at Wakefield in 1643, various letters, *etc., etc.*

CLAY, JOHN WILLIAM, ed. *Yorkshire Royalist composition papers, or, the proceedings of the Committee for Compounding with Delinquents during the Commonwealth.* Y.A.S., R.S. **15, 18 & 20**. 1893-6.

NUTTALL, W.L.F. 'The Yorkshire Commissioners appointed for the trial of King Charles the First', *Y.A.J.* **43**, 1971, 147-57. Brief biographies.

NEWTON, S.C. 'The pipe roll of a Cromwellian sheriff of Yorkshire', *Y.A.J.* **41**, 1966, 108-16. 1654.

DUCKETT, GEORGE, SIR. 'King James the Second's proposed repeal of the penal laws and Test Act in 1688: his question to the magistracy and corporations touching the same, with their answers thereto, in the three Ridings of Yorkshire', *Y.A.J.* **5**, 1879, 433-73. Gives many names of J.Ps, *etc.*

'The rebellion of 1745: accounts, correspondence, and muster rolls of the Yorkshire Association, in the possession of the Archbishop of York', *Northern genealogist* **3**, 1900, 17-24. Includes many names.

'Yorkshire assizes coroners' inquests 1858-1861 held at Doncaster', *F.S.* **18**(2), 1997, 66. Lists inquests held.

D. Quarter Sessions Records, etc.

PUTNAM, BERTHA HAVEN, ed. *Yorkshire sessions of the peace, 1361-1364.* Y.A.S., R.S. **100**. 1939.

WALKER, SIMON. 'Yorkshire justices of the peace 1389-1413', *English historical review* **108**(427), 1993, 281-313. Includes many names.

East Riding

FORSTER, G.C.F. *The East Riding Justices of the Peace in the seventeenth century.* E.Y.L.H.S. **30**. 1973. General discussion of their work.

North Riding

Detailed listings and discussions of quarter session records are provided in:

'North Riding Quarter Sessions records. Part 1. Administrative records', *North Riding Record Office report* 1968, 11-38. Calendar.

'The North Riding Quarter Sessions records. Part II. Records enrolled, registered, deposited or returned', *North Riding Record Office report* 1969, 25-48.

'The North Riding Quarter Sessions records. Part IV. The Justices of the Peace', *North Riding Record Office report* 1970, 21-3.

'The North Riding Quarter Sessions records. Part V. The court in session', *North Riding Record Office report* 1970, 23-8.

'The North Riding Quarter Sessions records. Part VI. Finance', *North Riding Record Office report* 1970, 29-40.

See also:

JEAFFRESON, JOHN CORDY. 'The manuscripts of the Lord Lieutenant and Justices of the Peace of the North Riding of Yorkshire', in *Ninth report of the Royal Commission on Historical Manuscripts, Part 1. Report and appendix.* H.M.S.O., 1883, 329-49. Includes 'list of the persons presented for recusancy at General Sessions held at Thirsk, 24 February 1690', listing 1,755 names; also many abstracts of deeds, *etc., etc.*

Many original records are printed in:

ATKINSON, J.C., ed. *Quarter sessions records.* North Riding Record Society **1-9**. 1884-92. 17-18th c., includes various lists of papists, oaths taken, *etc.* Extensive.

There are a number of discussions of the justices and their work:

FORSTER, G.C.F. 'The North Riding justices and their sessions, 1603-1625', *N.H.* **10**, 1975, 102-25.

COCKBURN, J.S. 'The North Riding justices, 1690-1750: a study in local administration', *Y.A.J.* **41**, 1962, 481-515.

WINT, HILARY. 'Cleveland and Teesside history among the North Riding Quarter Sessions records', *C.T.L.H.S.B.* **2**, 1968, 3-6; **3**, 1968, 9-11; **4**, 1969, 18-20; **5**, 1969, 17-19; **6**, 1969, 16-18; **10**, 1970, 17-18; **13**, 1971, 12-14.

West Riding

A detailed guide to West Riding Quarter Sessions records is provided by:

BARBER, B.J. *Guide to the Quarter Sessions records of the West Riding of Yorkshire, 1637-1971, and other official records.* Wakefield: West Yorkshire Archive Consultative Council, 1984.

See also:

JEAFFRESON, JOHN CORDY. 'Manuscripts of the West Riding of Yorkshire', in *Ninth report of the Royal Commission on Historical Manuscripts, Part 1. Report and appendix.* H.M.S.O., 1883, 324-9. Includes 'schedule of Catholics having real estate in the West Riding in or between the years 1717 and 1734', listing 229 names.

Full editions of a few records are available:

LISTER, JOHN, ed. *West Riding sessions rolls 1597/8-1602, prefaced by certain proceedings in the Court of the Lord President and Council of the North in 1595.* Y.A.S., R.S. **3**. 1888.

LISTER, JOHN, ed. *West Riding sessions records, vol.II. Orders, 1611-1642; indictments, 1637-1642.* Y.A.S., R.S. **54**. 1915.

BARBER, FAIRLESS. 'The West Riding sessions rolls', *Y.A.J.* **5**, 1879, 362-405. Extracts from order book, 1638.

[TURNER], J.H. 'Ancient session notes, extracted from the originals', *Y.N.Q.I.* **1**, 1888, *passim.* Continued in *Y.C.M.* **1**, 1891, 342-9; **3**, 1893, 47-53. Late 17th c., from the West Riding Quarter Sessions records.

J.Ps are listed in:

HOPKINSON, G.G. 'A list of South Yorkshire Justices of the Peace, 1745-[1888]', *T. Hunter A.S.* **8**(3), 1961, 163-5; **8**(4), 1962, 238-41.

'West Riding magistracy: new appointments', *Y.N.Q.I.* **3**, 1907, 340-41. List of names newly added in 1907.

For discussion of an earlier period, see:

ARNOLD, CAROL. 'The Commission of the Peace for the West Riding of Yorkshire, 1437-1509', in POLLARD, TONY, ed. *Property and politics: essays in later medieval history.* Gloucester: Alan Sutton, 1984, 116-38.

In 1889, county councils took over many of the functions of Quarter Sessions. A history of the West Riding County Council is available:

BARBER, B.J. & BERESFORD, M.W. *The West-Riding County Council, 1889-1974: historical studies.* Wakefield: West Yorkshire Metropolitan County Council, 1979. Includes list of Councillors in 1974.

E. *Liberty of St. Peter of York*

This 'liberty' covered 168 places in Yorkshire and elsewhere, and gave jurisdiction in matters of criminal and civil law to the Dean and Chapter of York Minster. This jurisdiction is discussed, with a list of the places covered, in:

LEAK, ADRIAN. *The Liberty of St. Peter of York 1800-1838.* Borthwick paper **77**. 1990.

2. RECORDS OF PAROCHIAL AND LOCAL GOVERNMENT

The records of local government – accounts of overseers and churchwardens, rate lists, settlement examinations, *etc.* – contain a great deal of information valuable to the genealogist. They frequently provide the names of the humble mass of the people whose names otherwise went unrecorded. An interesting selection of these documents is printed in:

PURVIS, J.S. *Tudor parish documents of the Diocese of York: a selection, with introduction and notes.* Cambridge: Cambridge University Press, 1948.

East Riding parish records are fully listed in:

BARLEY, M.W., ed. *Parochial documents of the Archdeaconry of the East Riding: an inventory.* Y.A.S., R.S. **99**. 1939.

For North Riding churchwardens' accounts, see:

JAQUES, HUGH. 'North Yorkshire churchwardens' accounts in the 18th century', *Journal* **6**; N.Y.C.R.O.P. **17**, 1976, 59-109. General discussion with extracts from Skipton accounts, and list of accounts at North Yorkshire County Record Office.

For general discussions of the operation of the poor law, see:

MITCHELSON, N. *The old poor law in East Yorkshire.* E.Y.L.H.S. **2**. 1953.

HASTINGS, R.P. *Poverty and the poor law in the North Riding of Yorkshire, c.1780-1837.* Borthwick papers **61**. 1982. Discussion.

Many documents relating to the poor law in the East Riding are printed in:

FALLOWFIELD, MARGARET, & WATSON, IAN, eds. *The new poor law in Humberside.* Hull: Humberside College of Higher Education, Local History Archives Unit, 1986. Collection of documents relating to the East Riding.

Aldborough

LAWSON-TANCRED, THOMAS, SIR, & WALKER, J.W., eds. 'Aldburgh with Boroughbridge. Liberty and Soc of Aldburgh near Boroughbridge, 6 Elizabeth (1563)', in *Miscellanea* **2**. Y.A.S., R.S. **74**. 1929. Record of a sheriff's tourn (court).

Allertonshire

NEWMAN, CHRISTINE M. 'Local court administration within the Liberty of Allertonshire, 1470-1540', *Archives* 22(93), 1995, 13-24. General study.

Attercliffe

FUREY, MARGARET. 'Settlement certificates from other parishes or townships to Attercliffe', *F.S.* 10(3), 1990, 77; 10(4), 1990, 98; 11(1), 1990, 14-15; 11(2), 1990, 40-41. Also includes certificates of paupers removed from Attercliffe, and other records.

Barningham

'Inventory of documents in the church safe, Barningham', *Teasdale Record Society* 6, 1941, 15-16. List of parish records.

Beverley

HISTORICAL MANUSCRIPTS COMMISSION. *Report on the manuscripts of the Corporation of Beverley.* H.M.S.O., 1900.

LEACH, ARTHUR F., ed. *Beverley town documents.* Selden Society 14. 1900. Medieval-16th c.

DENNETT, J., ed. *Beverley borough records, 1575-1821.* Y.A.S., R.S. 84. 1933.

MACMAHON, K.A., ed. *Beverley Corporation minute books, 1707-1835.* Y.A.S., R.S. 122. 1958.

MILLS, JAMES. 'Catalogue of a selection from the muniments of the Corporation of Beverley', *Y.C.M.* 1, 1891, 316-7.

SHERWOOD, GEO. F. TUDOR. 'Beverley: a list of all the persons that paid scot and lott in the town of Beverley, anno MCCCCLVJ', *Y.G.* 2, 1890, 289-91.

WITTY, J.R. 'Documents relating to Beverley and district', *Y.A.J.* 36, 1944-7, 338-48. Extracts from the private hand-book of the Common Clerk, relating to official business, 1728.

Bingley

'Bingley Workhouse', *K.D.F.H.S.J.* Winter 1996, 20. Census 1841.

Bradfield

ADDY, VALERIE. 'Bradfield poor law strays', *H. & D.F.H.S.J.* 9(2), 1996, 25-6.

MEREDITH, ROSAMUND. 'Bradfield civil parish records: a preliminary report', *National Register of Archives South Yorkshire Committee bulletin* 7, 1975, 11-13.

NEWTON, ROY. *Bradfield poor law documents.* 2 fiche. Sheffield: Sheffield and District F.H.S., 1994.

Bradford

CUDWORTH, WILLIAM. *Historical notes on the Bradford Corporation, with records of the lighting and watching commissioners and board of highway surveyors.* Bradford: Thomas Brear, 1881.

CUDWORTH, W. 'Bradford churchwardens (compiled from the parish church records)', *B.A.* N.S. 2, 1905, 297-9. List, 1667-1903.

KENZIE, K. 'Names from an assessment of Bradford inhabitants, 10 Nov 1749', *Bodkin* 15, 1989, 5; 16, 1989, 7. Presumably a parish rate.

WROOT, HERBERT E., ed. 'Bradford parish churchwardens' accounts', *B.A.* N.S. 1, 1900, 470-90. 1607-78.

WROOT, HERBERT E. 'The Bradford parish churchwardens' accounts', *B.A.* 2, 1895, 260-70. Extracts, 16-17th c.

'Bradford Militia assessments, June and September, 1716', *B.A.* N.S., 2, 1905, 98-105 & 135-41. Rate list.

'Bradford in 1759', *B.A.* 2, 1895, 216-7. Lists members of an association formed to detect felons.

'Were they in the Bradford Infirmary? 1851 census', *Bod-kin* 6, 1987, 6.

KENZIE, KEN. 'Were they in the poorhouse? 1851 census return for Bradford poorhouse', *Bod-kin* 3, 1986, 4-6.

Brighouse

See Hipperholme

Brodsworth

WHITING, C.E. 'The clerk's book, Brodsworth', *T. Hunter A.S.* 7, 1957, 30-35. Brief discussion.

Burnsall

STAVERT, W.J., ed. *The churchwardens' accounts of the parish of Burnsall-in-Craven, 1704-1769.* Skipton: Craven Herald, 1899.

Clayton

'Clayton in Bradford-Dale: town's officers', *Y.G.* **2**, 1890, 105-6. Lists overseers, road surveyors, land tax officers, constables and churchwardens, 1747-60.

'Work House: Clayton Workhouse (North Bierley Union) 1851 census RG9/3338', *Bod-kin* **8**, 1987, 4-6.

Cleveland

MINNS, VALERIE. 'Cleveland people in the settlement examinations, Kesteven, Lincs., Quarter Sessions 1700-1847', *J.Cl.F.H.S.* 7(4), 1998, 41-2.

Cottingham

WHITEHOUSE, JOHN. *Cottingham's care of its poor to 1834.* Cottingham local history series **1**. Cottingham: Cottingham Local History Society, 1970. General discussion.

Cowling

'From an all poor rate book: necessities for the poor of Cowling for the year 1750', *B.A.* **6**; N.S., **4**, 1921, 134. Brief extract.

Craven

HOYLE, RICHARD, ed. *Lord Thanet's benefaction to the poor of Craven in 1685.* Settle: Friends of Giggleswick Parish Records, 1978. Lists poor recipients.

Croft

MUNBY, LIONEL M. 'One that got away: Croft, a church that was not restored', *Local historian* **21**, 1991, 120-5. Discussion of a parochial dispute, 1869-73.

Dickering Wapentake

MIDDLETON, IRIS. 'A bill of all the free holders in Dickering, that have £10 per annum', *B.T.* **21**, 1985, 20-21.

Doncaster

BRENT, ANDREW, ed. *Doncaster borough courtier, volume one.* Doncaster: Waterdale Press, 1994. Text of a municipal memoranda book, 1568-1626. Extensive.

LINDLEY, PAMELA. *Freemen of the Borough of Doncaster, 1558-1974.* 2 vols. Doncaster: Doncaster & District F.H.S., 1998.

HARDY, WILLIAM J., ed. *A calendar to the records of the Borough of Doncaster.* 4 vols. Doncaster: Corporation of Doncaster, 1899-1903. Contents: v.1. Royal charters & ancient title deeds. v.2. Court rolls of Doncaster, Rossington, Hexthorpe, and Long Sandall. v.3. Court rolls of Doncaster, volumes V-X. v.4. Courtiers of the Corporation.

JACKSON, CHARLES. *Doncaster charities, past and present.* Worksop: Robert White, 1881. Includes many pedigrees.

MARTIN, G.H., et al. *Doncaster: a borough and its charters: Five essays.* Doncaster: Waterdale Press, 1994. Contents: MARTIN, G.H. 'Doncaster borough charters'. DANBURY, E.A. 'The decoration of the Doncaster borough charters'. GOLDBERG, P.J.P. 'From Conquest to Corporation'. BARBER, B.J. 'The Corporation and the community'. BERESFORD, M.W. 'In pursuit of the medieval boroughs of the West Riding'. BARBER, B.J. 'Doncaster borough charters, 1194-1836: an abstract'.

Ecclesall Bierlow Union

TURTON, L.M.J. 'Residents of the Ecclesall Bierlow Union Workhouse', *F.S.* 3(3), 1982, 70-71; 3(4), 1982, 87; 4(1), 1982, 16-17. Extracted from the 1851 census.

Ecclesfield

WINDER, THOMAS. 'Surveyors of the highways in the lower division of Ecclesfield', *T. Hunter A.S.* 2(2), 1921, 159-64. Discussion of surveyors' accounts, 1812-23.

Elland

HAMER, S.H. 'Extracts from some Elland records, 1729-1804', *P.R.H.A.S.* 1907, 13-34. Extracts from churchwardens' accounts.

CROSSLEY, E.W. 'The Elland churchwardens' accounts', *P.R.H.A.S.* 1927, 157-83; 1929, 305-29. Discussion, 17-18th c.

Guisborough

O'SULLIVAN, D. 'Guisborough Hospital and the Pursgloves', *C.T.L.H.S.B.* **47**, 1984, 20-28. Almshouses. Includes extract from accounts of rent, 1575/6, and pedigree of Pursglove, 16-17th c.

'Guisborough poor in the 18th and 19th centuries', *North Riding Record Office report* 1967, 15-21.

Halifax

BETTERIDGE, ALAN. 'Halifax before the Industrial Revolution: a study of local administrative records, 1585-1762', *T. Hal. A.S.* 1978, 17-41; 1979, 81-103.

BRETTON, R. 'Settlement certificates and removal orders', *T. Hal. A.S.* 1959, 9-26. For Halifax.

HANSON, T.W. 'The minutes of Halifax Workhouse (1635 to 1704)', *P.R.H.A.S.* 1921, 77-96. Extracts; not a full transcript.

HOUSEMAN, J.W. 'Notes and comments on Halifax churchwardens' accounts, 1620-1714', *P.R.H.A.S.* 1925, 137-67.

HOUSEMAN, J.W. 'Notes and comments on Halifax churchwardens' accounts, 1714-1800', *P.R.H.A.S.* 1925, 109-39.

HOUSEMAN, J.W. 'Further notes and comments on the Halifax churchwardens' accounts, 1714-1832', *P.R.H.A.S.* 1927, 77-100.

HOUSEMAN, J.W. 'The development of local government in the parish of Halifax, 1760-1848', *T. Hal. A.S.* 1929, 117-207. Includes lists of officers at Northowram and Skircoat.

Hipperholme

HOUSEMAN, J.W. 'Local township records: Hipperholme-cum-Brighouse, 1813-1829', *T. Hal. A.S.* 1930, 77-110.

T., J.H. 'Greves, graves or prepositi', *Y.G.* **1**, 1888, 34-9, 64-6 & 203-8; **2**, 1890, 46-51; **3**, 1893, 38-40. Lists greaves of Hipperholme, Rastrick and Scammonden in the manor of Wakefield, medieval-1655.

Honley

JAGGER, MRS. 'Churchwardens of Honley', *Y.C.M.* **1**, 1891, 172-4. List, 17-19th c.

Hooton Pagnel

WHITING, C.E., ed. *The accounts of the churchwardens, constables, overseers of the poor, and overseers of the highways of the parish of Hooton Pagnel, 1767-1820.* Y.A.S., R.S. **97**. 1938.

Hornby

BOULTBEE, MARY A. *Gleanings from an iron chest in the church of St. Mary's, Hornby.* Darlington: Wm. Dresser & Sons, 1901.

Horton

'Assessment for raising a force of cavalry, Horton township, 1798, Division of Morley in the W.R. of York', *B.A.* N.S. **1**, 1900, 111-12.

Howden

BINGHAM, DORIAN M. 'Howden', *B.T.* **29**, 1987, 17-19. Includes extract from Howden poor book, 1801, and 1851 census, *etc.*

Huddersfield

'Other genealogical sources', *H. & D.F.H.S.J.* 2(2), 1989, 34. Facsimile of 'the names of all the poor in Huddersfield parish', 1612.

'Other genealogical sources', *H. & D.F.H.S.J.* 3(2), 1990, 32. Facsimile of a page from Huddersfield overseers' account book, 1769.

Hull

LAMBERT, J. MALET. *Two thousand years of gild life, or, an outline of the history and development of the gild system from early times, with special reference to its application to trade and industry, together with a full account of the gilds and trading companies of Kingston-upon-Hull, from the 14th to the 18th century.* Hull: A. Brown & Sons, 1891. The Hull material occupies two-thirds of the book; includes notes on memorials.

STANEWELL, L.M., ed. *Calendar of the ancient-deeds, letters, miscellaneous old documents, &c., in the archives of the Corporation.* Hull: City and County of Kingston upon Hull, 1951.

WILDRIDGE, T. TINDALL. *Hull's honour roll, being a list of all the municipal dignitaries and officers of the borough from its establishment to the present time.* Hull: Montgomery & Son, 1891.

'Bastardy orders and recognizances from Hull Quarter Sessions', *B.T.* **16**, 1983, 16-19. 1786-1800.

Keighley Union
'Nominations for guardians of the poor, Keighley Union, 1849 to 1865', *K.D.F.H.S.J.* Spring 1999, 8-9.

Lackenby
DIXON, GRACE. 'The ancient charity of John Jackson of Lackenby', *Cleveland history* **70**, 1996, 40-46. Includes pedigree of Jackson and King, 18-19th c.

Leeds
'A brawl in Kirkgate, 13 Edward II', in *Miscellanea* [2]. *T.S.* **4**, 1895, 125-38. Transcript of a case in the *Coram Rege* rolls.

KIRBY, JOAN W. 'The rulers of Leeds: gentry, clothiers and merchants, c.1425-1626', *Miscellany* **18**. T.S. **59**, 1985, 22-49. Includes list of the Corporation in 1626.

KIRBY, JOAN W. 'A Leeds elite: the principal burgesses of the first Leeds corporation', *N.H.* **20**, 1984, 88-107. Includes biographical notes on principal burgesses and assistants in 1626.

LUMB, G.D. 'St. John's church, Leeds: the trustees (feoffees) account book, 1660-1766', in *Miscellanea* [7]. *T.S.* **24**, 1919, 379-98.

KIRBY, JOAN W. 'Restoration Leeds and the aldermen of the corporation, 1661-1700', *N.H.* **22**, 1986, 123-74.

CLARK, J.G., ed. *The court book of the Leeds Corporation. First book. January 1662 to August 1705.* T.S. **34**. 1936.

'The Committee of Charitable Uses, Leeds: extracts from the minute-book commencing 1664', in *Miscellanea* [6.] *T.S.* **22**, 1915, 364-86.

ANDERSON, PHILIP. 'The Leeds Workhouse under the old poor law 1762-1834', *Thoresby miscellany* **17**. T.S. **56**, 1981, 75-113. Gives the names of the many employers of George Orange and Joseph Richardson, 1818-20.

SKELTON, SANDY. 'Poor Law Union: Leeds minute books', *Y.F.H.* **20**(2), 1994, 48-9. Extracts of orders for 1865.

Methley
CLARK, E. KITSON. 'Churchwardens' accounts, Methley', in *Miscellanea* [4]. *T.S.* **11**, 1904, 236-80. Detailed discussion, with transcript of accounts, 1681-1705, by H. Armstrong Hall.

Middlesbrough
NICHOLSON, J.T. *Middlesbrough Workhouse. Census returns 1881; census returns 1891.* [ ]: [Cleveland F.H.S.], [199-].

Middlesbrough Workhouse 1881 census. [ ]: Cleveland F.H.S., [199-]. 'Volume 3' on cover.

Middlesbrough Workhouse 1891 census. [ ]: Cleveland F.H.S., [199-]. 'Volume 1' on cover.

NICHOLSON, J.T. *Middlesbrough. Nazareth House census returns 1891.* [ ]: [Cleveland F.H.S.], [199-].

Middleton Tyas
MCLEE, CAROL. 'The Christmas bonus', *J.Cl.F.H.S.* **6**(1), 1995, 24-7. List of poor at Middleton Tyas, 1780.

Midgley
HARWOOD, H.W. 'Midgley records', *T. Hal. A.S.* 1942, 139-50. 18-19th c.

HARWOOD, H.W. 'Midgley township records, 1739 to 1769', *T. Hal. A.S.* 1940, 119-45; 1941, 57-70.

Moor Monkton
'List of overseers of the poor, surveyors of the highways, constables and churchwardens', *Y.A.S., F.H.P.S.S.N.* **7**, 1974, 5. For Moor Monkton, 1731-1841 (surnames only, individual dates not given).

Morley
'Churchwardens', *Cameo* 1995, no.1, 7; no.2, 7; no.3, 12. For Morley, 1700-1775.

'Morley mayors, 1886-1932', *Cameo* 1993, no.2, 12. List.

Nether Hallam
WINDER, THOS. 'An old 'Hallam Nether' rate book (1780-1797)', *T. Hunter A.S.* **1**(1), 1914, 86-90. General discussion, with extracts, of rate book of Nether Hallam.

North Bierley Union
See Clayton

Penistone
SHORTLAND, TED. 'Inmates of Penistone Workhouse', *F.S.* **6**(4), 1986, 94.

Pontefract

JEAFFRESON, JOHN CORDY. 'Manuscripts of the Corporation of the Borough of Beverley', in *Eighth report of the Royal Commission on Historical Manuscripts, appendix, Part 1 (section II)*. H.M.S.O., 1881, 269-76.

HOLMES, RICHARD. *The booke of entries of the Pontefract Corporation, 1653-1726.* Collections towards the history of Pontefract 1. Pontefract: Richard Holmes, 1882.

The mayors of the Borough of Pontefract from the incorporation in 1484, with partial lists of the aldermen. Pontefract: J.O.E. Holmes, 1993.

Rastrick

'Graves of Rastrick', *T. Hal. A.S.* 1943, 121-2. List of officeholders, 1274-1340.

See also Hipperholme

Richmond

WENHAM, L.P., ed. *Richmond Municipal Reform Association: minute books 1841-1859.* N.Y.C.R.O.P. **19**. 1978. Includes list of members 1841, list of mayors, aldermen and councillors, 1835-60, and list of assessors and auditors, 1835-1859.

Ripon

'Poor relief in Ripon', *Journal* **1**; N.Y.C.R.O.P. **1**, 1975, 41-50.

Rotherham

BUGLER, J.R. 'Records of the feoffees of the common lands of Rotherham', *National Register of Archives South Yorkshire Committee bulletin* **2**, 1960, 3-4. Brief discussion.

MACKENZIE, MARGARET H. 'The early papers of the Rotherham feoffees', *T. Hunter A.S.* **10**(5), 1979, 350-59. 16-18th c.

Saddleworth

FOX, MICHAEL. 'Records of the Saddleworth Friendly Family Burial Society', *B.S.H.S.* **21**(3), 1991, 8-14.

H., J.M. 'Some local settlement certificates, 1697-1741', *B.S.H.S.* **13**(3), 1983, 62-4. List of Saddleworth certificates.

Scammonden

See Hipperholme

Scarborough

ASHCROFT, M.Y., ed. *Scarborough records, 1600-1640: a calendar.* N.Y.C.R.O.P. **47**. 1991. Extensive calendar of borough records.

FORSTER, G.C.F. *A descriptive catalogue of the records in the possession of the Corporation of Scarborough.* Scarborough: the Borough, 1968.

FORSTER, G.C.F. 'The records of Scarborough to 1835', *Scarborough and District Archaeological Society transactions* **1**(1), 1958, 10-19.

JEAYES, ISAAC HERBERT. *Catalogue of ancient documents belonging to the Corporation of Scarborough.* [Scarborough]: [The Corporation], 1915.

JEAYES, ISAAC H., ed. *Description of documents contained in the white vellum book of the Scarborough Corporation.* Scarborough: Geo. A. Pinder & Son, 1914.

Selby

'Presentments of the juries at the courts of the Abbot of Selby', in R[AINE], J., [junior], ed. *A volume of English miscellanies illustrating the history and language of the northern counties of England.* Surtees Society **85**, 1890, 22-34. 1472-1533.

Sinnington

GREEN, R. 'Administration of the poor law in Sinnington', *Y.F.H.* **20**(3), 1994, 67-9. Includes extracts from minutes, 1821-8.

Sheffield

INCE, T.N. 'Constables' duties at Sheffield in 1650', *Reliquary* **5**, 1864-5, 23-5. Includes extracts from constables' accounts; also notes on Fox family.

LEADER, JOHN DANIEL. *Extracts from the earliest book of accounts belonging to the town trustees of Sheffield, dating from 1566 to 1707, with explanatory notes.* Sheffield: Leader & Sons, 1879.

LEADER, JOHN DANIEL, ed. *The records of the Burgery of Sheffield, commonly called the Town Trust, with introduction and notes.* Elliot Stock, 1897. Extensive transcripts of accounts, minutes, *etc.*, 16-19th c.

SHAW, EDWIN. *A biographical register of the Sheffield town trustees, September 1681-July 1967.* Sheffield: Greenup & Thompson, 1967.

WALLIS, P.J. 'Sheffield church burgesses: a biographical register', *T. Hunter A.S.* **7**, 1957, 51-62, 144-57, 194-9 & 344-58. Biographical dictionary.

WALTON, MARY. 'The stock of the town of Sheffield', *T. Hunter A.S.* **4**, 1937, 252-9. Includes list of the town's 'poor', 1603.

HOBSON, FRED. 'Gentlemen constables for Sheffield', *F.S.* **12**(1), 1991, 19-22. List of 100 constables appointed 1812; also lists for Brightside Bierlow and Nether Hallam.

Sheffield Union

WILDE, ELAINE. 'Sheffield Union workhouse', *F.S.* **13**(1), 1992, 9. Plaque listing guardians who served durig the erection and opening of the workhouse.

WILDE, ELAINE. 'Sheffield Union Fir Vale House: names of guardians comprising the Board on the 31st March, *anno* 1930 *domini*', *F.S.* **13**(1), 1992, 10.

Shelf

BARRETT, F. 'Local government in Shelf, 1700-1937', *T. Hal. A.S.* 1979, 9-53; 1980, 27-62. Includes list of overseers, 1713-1828, and extracts from parish records with many names.

HOUSEMAN, J.W. 'Local township records: Shelf, 1714-1841', *T. Hal. A.S.* 1932, 293-314.

Sheriff Hutton

PURVIS, J.S. 'The churchwardens' book of Sheriff Hutton. A.D. 1524-1568', *Y.A.J.* **36**, 1944-7, 178-89. Extracts.

Shipley

'A Shipley document 1688', *Y.N.Q.II.* **2**, 1906, 138. See also **4**, 1908, 7-8. List of freeholders and inhabitants, for constables' assessment.

Skipton

'Inmates of Skipton Workhouse, Gargrave Road, 1881 census', *K.D.F.H.S.J.* Spring 1992, 4. Surnames only.

Skircoat

BRETTON, R. 'Skircoat township minute book', *T. Hal. A.S.* 1957, 41-63. Includes list of constables.

South Stockton

COMONT, SUSAN. 'The archives of the South Stockton Local Board and Thornaby Borough Council', *C.T.L.H.S.B.* **35**, 1978, 25-7.

Southowram

PORRITT, A. 'The Southowram Workhouse', *T. Hal. A.S.* 1961, 1-14. 18-19th c.

Sowerby

KENDALL, H.P. 'Sowerby constables' accounts', *P.R.H.A.S.* 1902 & 1903 (unpaginated); 1904-5, 129-41 & 177-86; 1906, 17-32. 17th c.

SMITH, A. 'Some Sowerby constables' accounts', *T. Hal. A.S.* 1957, 19-35.

SMITH, ARNOLD. 'Sowerby constables' accounts, 1715-1867', *T. Hal. A.S.* 1964, 41-57.

Soyland

PRIESTLEY, J.H. 'The growth of a township: Soyland', *T. Hal. A.S.* 1955, 33-46. Based on parish records; includes assessments of 1675 and 1693.

Thornaby

See South Stockton

Thornhill

HARISTY, OWEN. 'The names of those that have contributed within ye parish of Thornhill towards the building of St. Poules in London', *Y.F.H.* **14**(4), 1988, 92-3. Collection taken by the churchwardens, undated but presumably late 17th c.

Thornton

Thornton churchwardens' book, 1684-1800. Bradford: Brian Jones, 1999. Not seen

Todmorden

HOLDEN, JOSHUA. 'Township records in the Todmorden district', *P.R.H.A.S.* 1908, 1-22.

Wakefield

WALKER, J.W., ed. 'The burgess court, Wakefield, 1533, 1554, 1556 and 1579', in *Miscellanea* **2**. Y.A.S., R.S. **74**. 1929, 16-32.

Warley

SUTCLIFFE, T. 'Extracts from old Warley township accounts', *P.R.H.A.S.* 1907, 37-64. Late 18th c.

Westerdale

'Constable Barker's papers', *J.Cl.F.H.S.* 5(6), 1993, 32-5. Of Westerdale; includes window tax assessment 1796, lists of tithe rents, 1759 and 1787, militia list 1762, *etc.*

Whitby

'A panic about phanatics 1679', *J.Cl.F.H.S.* 4(11), 1991, 26-7. Certificate of some parishioners of Whitby regarding their schoolmaster, Christopher Stephenson.

Whitkirk

PLATT, GEO. MORETON. 'Collections made in the parish church of Whitkirk, Yorkshire, 1661-1679', in *Miscellanea* 1. *T.S.* 2, 1891, 142-8.

Wortley Union

SHORTLAND, J.E. 'Inmates of the Wortley Union Workhouse, 1871', *F.S.* 6(1), 1985, 22-3; 6(2), 1985, 40-41.

Wressell

'An assessment laid on the inhabitants of the parish of Wressell ...', *B.T.* 25, 1986, 17. For 1806.

York

A. *Officers*

KIGHTLY, CHARLES, & SEMLYEN, RACHEL. *Lords of the City: the lord mayors of York and their mansion house.* York: York City Council, 1980. Includes list of lord mayors, 13-20th c.

A list or catalogue of all the mayors and bayliffs, lord mayors and sheriffs, of the most ancient, honourable, noble and loyal City of York from the time of King Edward I to the year 1664 ... Jonas Browne, [1715.] Originally published York: Stephen Bulkley, 1664.

MURRAY, HUGH. 'The mayor's esquires', *York historian* 6, 1985, 3-23. Biographical notes on York city sergeants (1314-1378), mace bearers (1389-1980) and sword bearers (1389-1983).

B. *City Records*

GILES, WILLIAM. *Catalogue of the charters, house books, freemen's rolls, chamberlains' accounts, etc., and other books, deeds, and all documents belonging to the Corporation of York, together with a report on their renovation.* York: The Corporation, 1908.

RILEY, HENRY THOMAS. 'The Corporation of the City of York' in *First report of the Royal Commission on Historical Manuscripts.* H.M.S.O., 1874, 108-10. Brief survey of the Corporation's archives.

'Verdicts of the searchers called in to decide about encroachments, *etc.,* in the City of York', in R[AINE], J., [junior], ed. *A volume of English miscellanies illustrating the history and language of the northern counties of England.* Surtees Society 85, 1890, 11-22. 1417-1501.

PALLISER, D.M. 'York's earliest administrative record: the husgabel roll of c.1284', *Y.A.J.* 50, 1978, 81-91. A 'husgabel' was a tax on house properties paid to the king; this roll lists 373 taxpayers.

DOBSON, R.B. *York City chamberlains' account rolls, 1396-1500.* Surtees Society 192. 1980. Includes list of 'mayors and chamberlains of the City of York, 1396-1500'.

DAVIES, ROBERT. *Extracts from the municipal records of the City of York, during the reigns of Edward IV, Edward V and Richard III.* J.B. Nichols and Son, 1843. Reprinted as *York records of the fifteenth century.* Dursley: Gloucester Reprints, 1976.

SKAIFE, ROBERT H. 'Extracts from the house books of the Corporation of York', *Y.A.J.* 14, 1896-7, 444-57. Includes biographical notes on persons mentioned.

JOHNSTON, ALEXANDRA F., & ROGERSON, MARGARET. *Records of early English drama: York.* 2 vols. Manchester University Press, 1979. Includes extensive extracts from York civic records, with many names; also list of 'Pageant masters of the Mercers' Guild'.

PRESTWICH, MICHAEL. *York civic ordinances 1301.* Borthwick papers 49. 1976. Transcript; includes various lists of names.

S[ELLERS], M., ed. *York memorandum book.* 2 vols. Surtees Society **120** & **125**. 1912. Contents: Pt.1. 1376-1419. Pt.2. 1388-1493.

PERCY, JOYCE W., ed. *York memorandum book.* Surtees Society **186**. 1973. For 1371-1596.

ATTREED, LORRAINE C., ed. *York house books, 1461-1490.* 2 vols. Stroud: Alan Sutton, 1991. Supersedes the first volume of Angelo Raine's *York Civic records*.

RAINE, ANGELO, ed. *York civic records, vol.I.* Y.A.S., R.S. **98**. 1939. House books, 1474-1487.

RAINE, ANGELO, ed. *York civic records, vol. II.* Y.A.S., R.S. **103**. 1941. House books, 1487-1504.

RAINE, ANGELO, ed. *York civic records, vol. III.* Y.A.S., R.S. **106**. 1942. House books, 1504-36.

RAINE, ANGELO, ed. *York civic records, vol. IV.* Y.A.S., R.S. **108**. 1945. House books, 1536-48.

RAINE, ANGELO, ed. *York civic records, vol. V.* Y.A.S., R.S. **110**. 1946. 1548-58.

RAINE, ANGELO, ed. *York civic records, vol. VI.* Y.A.S., R.S. **112**. 1948. House books, 1558-69.

RAINE, ANGELO, ed. *York civic records, vol. VII.* Y.A.S., R.S. **115**. 1950. House books, 1569-78.

RAINE, ANGELO, ed. *York civic records, vol. VIII.* Y.A.S., R.S. **119**. 1953. House books, 1578-88.

SUTTON, DEBORAH, ed. *York civic records, vol. IX.* Y.A.S., R.S. **138**. 1978. House books, 1588-91.

'Certificates of the English parentage and birth of certain persons who have been charged with being Scots [from the York city records]', in R[AINE], J., [junior], ed. *A volume of English miscellanies illustrating the history and language of the northern counties of England.* Surtees Society **85**, 1890, 35-52.

FOWKES, JOYCE W. 'The minute book of the York court of Quarter Sessions, 1638-1662', *Y.A.J.* **41**, 1966, 449-54. Brief discussion.

RAINE, ANGELO, ed. 'Proceedings of the Commonwealth Committee for York and the Ainsty', in WHITING, C.E., ed. *Miscellanea* **6**. Y.A.S., R.S. **118**. 1953, 1-30.

C. *Freedom Registers*

DOBSON, R.B. 'Admissions to the freedom of the City of York in the later middle ages', *Economic history review* 2nd series **26**, 1973, 1-7. General discussion.

BAKES, STANLEY. 'A family tree for a York freeman', *Y.F.H.S.N.* **11**, 1985, 16-18. Discussion of records for freemen.

[COLLINS, FRANCIS], ed. *Register of the freemen of the City of York, from the city records.* 2 vols. Surtees Society **96** & **102**. 1897-1900. Contents: v.1. 1272-1558. v.2. 1559-1759. Corrected in:

PALLISER, D.M. 'The York freemen's register 1273-1540: amendments and additions', *York historian* **12**, 1995, 21-7.

See also:

MUGGLESTON, J. 'Some aspects of the two late medieval chamberlains' account books of York', *Y.A.J.* **67**, 1995, 133-46. Includes list of freemen admitted 1448-1451.

PALLISER, D.M. 'A regional capital as magnet: immigrants to York, 1477-1566', *Y.A.J.* **57**, 1985, 111-23. Includes 'Calendar of freeman admissions stating birthplaces', listing 271 names.

MALDEN, JOHN. *Register of York freemen 1680 to 1986.* York: William Sessions, 1989. The register itself is on 5 fiche.

D. *Guild Records*

'Gild records of York', *Yorkshire Architectural and York Archaeological Society annual report* 1948-9, 14-36. Catalogue of an exhibition.

[SCAIFE, ROBERT H.], ed. *The register of the Guild of Corpus Christi in the City of York, with an appendix of illustrative documents containing some account of the Hospital of St. Thomas of Canterbury, without Micklegate-Bar in the suburbs of the city.* Surtees Society **57**. 1872. Lists guild members, 15-16th c.

WHITE, EILEEN. *The St. Christopher and St. George Guild of York.* Borthwick paper **72**. 1987.

E. *Parish Records*
St. John the Evangelist

BRODE, T.A. 'Old parish account books of St. John the Evangelist, York', *Reports and papers of the Associated Architectural Societies* **29**(1), 1907, 304-22. Extracts, 1580-1800, with some names.

St. Martin cum Gregory

BENSON, GEORGE. 'Churchwardens' accounts of St. Martin-cum-Gregory, York', *Reports and papers of the Associated Architectural Societies* **31**(1), 1911, 303-18; **31**(2), 1912, 613-28. 1560-1754; not a transcript, but includes a few names.

St. Michael Spurriergate

WEBB, C.C., ed. *The churchwardens' accounts of St. Michael, Spurriergate, York, 1518-1548.* 2 vols. B.T.C. 20. York: Bk.I.H.R., 1997.

'Two hundred years of parish life in York', *Yorkshire Architectural and York Archaeological Society annual report and summary of proceedings* 1950-51, 17-58. Discussion of 16-17th c. churchwardens' books of Saint Michael Spurriergate, York, with extracts.

York Minster

'York Minster chamberlains' accounts and St. Peter's accounts: a summary list', *B.I.B.* 1, 1975-8, 43-8.

3. ECCLESIASTICAL RECORDS

The church formerly played a much more important role in society than it does today. Its courts exercised jurisdiction over beliefs and morals, and over probate; its clergy recorded births, marriages and deaths; its churchwardens played a major role in parish government. Consequently, ecclesiastical records are of major importance to genealogists, and publications based on them are listed throughout this bibliography. The focus of this chapter is on those publications directly concerned with the church itself, its administration, and its clergy. Parish registers and probate records are listed in *Yorkshire parish registers, monumental inscriptions and wills* (vol.2 of *Yorkshire: the genealogists library guide);* for churchwardens' accounts, see section 2 above; ecclesiastical estate records are listed in section 4E below, and tithe records may be found in section 4G.

A. *History of the Diocese of York, etc.*
There are a number of general histories of the Diocese:

ORNSBY, GEORGE. *York.* Diocesan histories. Society for Promoting Christian Knowledge, [1882].

BURTON, JOHN. *Monasticon Eboracense, and the ecclesiastical history of Yorkshire, containing an account of the first introduction and progress of Christianity in that diocese, untill the end of William the Conqueror's reign; also the description of the situation, fabric, times of endowments of all churches, collegiate, conventual, parochial or of earliar jurisdiction, and of other religious places in that district, and to whose memory they were dedicated; together with an account of such monuments and inscriptions as are worthy of notice, as well as of the rise, progress, establishment, privileges and suppression of each order fixed therein, with the catalogues of all the abbots and other superiors of those places, and of all the patrons, rectors, vicars, cantarists, &c., of each church, chapel &c., from the earliest account down to the present time ... with above two thousand copies of original charters and deeds never yet published ...* York: N. Nickson for the author, 1758.

CUMING, G.J., ed. *The Province of York: papers read at the fifth summer meeting of the Ecclesiastical History Society.* Studies in church history 4. Leiden: E.J. Brill, 1967. Collection of essays.

RAINE, JAMES, ed. *The historians of the church of York and its archbishops.* 3 vols. Rolls series **71**. Longman & Co., et al, 1879-94. Vol. 3 includes 176 letters and other medieval documents, with many names. The other volumes are primarily of Anglo-Saxon interest.

For surveys of churches, *etc.,* see:

LAWTON, GEORGE. *Collectio rerum ecclesiasticarum de Diocesi Eboracensi, or, collections relative to churches and chapels within the Diocese of York, to which are added, collections relative to churches and chapels within the Diocese of Ripon.* New ed. J.G.F. & J. Rivington, 1842. Parochial survey of churches.

HATTON, W.H., & FOX, W.E. *The churches of Yorkshire, illustrated, with full descriptions of their styles of architecture, extracts from the registers, historical facts, local customs, and events connected therewith.* Elliot Stock, 1879. Includes lists of clergy, notes on inscriptions, *etc., etc.*

For a study of the modern Diocese of Sheffield (formerly part of the York Diocese), see:

WALTON, MARY. *A history of the Diocese of Sheffield, 1914-1979.* Sheffield: Diocesan Board of Finance, 1981.

The activities of the ecclesiastical courts are discussed in:

RITCHIE, CARSON I.A. *The ecclesiastical courts of York.* Arbroath: Herald Press, 1956. General discussion of their activities.

PURVIS, J.S. 'The ecclesiastical courts of York', *Archives* 3(17), 1958, 18-27. Discussion of procedures and records *etc.*

A commonly overlooked source for genealogists are works dealing with church bells and plate. These frequently include the names of clergy, churchwardens, benefactors, makers, *etc.* See:

FALLOW, T.M., & MCCALL, H.B. *Yorkshire church plate.* 2 vols. Y.A.S. Extra series **3-4**. 1912-15. v.1. The City of York; the North Riding; the East Riding. v.2. The West Riding.

BOULTER, W. CONSITT. 'Inscriptions on church bells of the East Riding of Yorkshire', *Y.A.J.* **2**, 1873, 82-6, 215-25; **3**, 1875, 26-32 & 404-7.

POPPLETON, J. EYRE. 'Notes on the bells of the ancient churches in the West Riding of Yorkshire', *Y.A.J.* **17**, 1902-3, 1-32, 192-236 & 434-61; **18**, 1904-5, 88-104. Includes list of bellfounders.

POPPLETON, J. EYRE. 'Notes on the bells of the ancient churches of the West Riding', *Y.A.J.* **16**, 1900-1, 46-83. Many names of founders, churchwardens, benefactors, *etc.*

GREENWOOD, DENNIS. *The bells of the churches in the Diocese of Wakefield.* Huddersfield: Dennis Greenwood, 1995. Includes inscriptions found on bells, with many names of founders, benefactors, clergy, churchwardens, *etc.*

Other general works include:

COX, CHARLES. 'Sanctuaries and sanctuary seekers of Yorkshire', *Archaeological journal* **68**, 1911, 273-99. Mentions a few names.

PURVIS, J.S. 'A note on pews and stalls', *Y.A.J.* **37**, 1951, 162-94. Discussion of the right to a pew in church, with various extracts – and names – from cases in the ecclesiastical courts.

The 'peculiar' of York Minster included many parishes throughout Yorkshire. Its courts are described in:

BROWN, SANDRA. *The medieval courts of the York Minster peculiar.* Borthwick paper **66**. 1984. Includes lists of officers.

See also:

FALLOW, T.M. 'Some Elizabethan visitations of the churches belonging to the Peculiar of the Dean of York', *Y.A.J.* **18**, 1904-5, 197-232 & 313-41.

'York Minster Deanery causes and act books', *B.I.B.* **2**, 1979-82, 169-75. List.

A wide variety of books and articles dealing with specific periods of diocesan history are available; a selection of them is listed here in rough chronological order.

13-15th century

NEWMAN, J.E. 'Greater and lesser landowners and parochial patronage: Yorkshire in the thirteenth century', *English historical review* **92**, 1977, 280-308. Study of advowsons and their owners.

PEDERSEN, FREDERIC. 'Demography in the archives: social and geographical factors in fourteenth-century York cause paper marriage litigation', *Continuity and change* 10, 1995, 405-36. Based on York Diocesan cause papers.

PEDERSEN, FREDERIC. 'Did the medieval laity know the canon law rules on marriage? Some evidence from fourteenth-century York cause papers', *Medieval studies* 56, 1994, 111-52.

SWANSON, R.N. 'Papal letters among the ecclesiastical archives of York, 1378-1415', *B.I.B.* 1, 1975-8, 165-93. Transcripts, with many names.

16-18th century

DICKENS, A.G. *Reformation studies.* Hambledon, 1982. Collection of essays, including many on the reformation in Yorkshire.

DICKENS, A.G. *Lollards and protestants in the Diocese of York, 1509-1558.* Oxford University Press for the University of Hull, 1959.

DICKENS, A.G. *The Marian reaction in the Diocese of York.* 2 vols. St. Anthony's Hall publications 11-12. St. Anthony's Press, 1957. Pt.1. The clergy. Pt.2. The laity. Pt.1 includes a list of married clergy, and of institutions 1554-5.

MARCHANT, RONALD A. *The Church under the law: justice, administration, and discipline in the Diocese of York, 1560-1640.* Cambridge: C.U.P., 1969.

MARCHANT, RONALD A. *The Puritans and the church courts in the Diocese of York, 1560-1642.* Longmans, 1960.

SHARPE, J.A. *Defamation and sexual slander in early modern England: the church courts at York.* Borthwick papers 58. 1980.

CROSS, CLAIRE. 'Sin and society: the northern High Commission and the northern gentry in the time of Elizabeth I', in CROSS, CLAIRE, LOADES, DAVID M., & SCARISBRICK, J.J., eds. *Law and government under the Tudors: essays presented to Sir Geoffrey Elton, Regius professor of modern history in the University of Cambridge, on the occasion of his retirement.* Cambridge: Cambridge University Press, 1988, 195-209. Based on the High Commission act books.

CROSS, CLAIRE. 'The religious life of women in sixteenth-century Yorkshire', in SHEILS, W.J., & WOOD, DIANA, eds. *Women in the church.* Studies in church history 27. Oxford: Basil Blackwell for the Ecclesiastical History Society, 1990. 307-24.

ADDY, JOHN. *The Archdeacon and ecclesiastical discipline in Yorkshire, 1598-1714: clergy and the churchwardens.* St. Anthony's Hall publications 24. York: St. Anthony's Press, 1963.

19-20th century

'The formation of new parishes and ecclesiastical districts in the Diocese of York 1818-1968: a summary list', *B.I.B.* 2, 1979-82, 27-59. Lists new parishes.

B. *Published Sources*

Many of the major sources for the history of York Diocese have been edited for publication; these record publications are listed here. Works dealing solely with the clergy are listed in section D below, although many of the items listed here also include relevant material.

Eleventh and twelfth century *Acta* are printed in:

BURTON, JANET E., ed. *English episcopal acta V: York 1070-1154.* Oxford: Oxford University Press, 1988.

The major source for the history of the medieval diocese are the bishops' registers. These are discussed in:

JACOB, ERNEST FRASER. *The medieval registers of Canterbury and York.* St. Anthony's Hall publications 4. St. Anthony's Press, 1953.

THOMPSON, A. HAMILTON. 'The registers of the Archbishops of York: an address ... ', *Y.A.J.* 32, 1936, 245-63.

Many extracts from bishops' registers are printed in:

RAINE, JAMES, ed. *Historical papers and letters from the northern registers.* Rolls series. 61. Longman & Co., 1873. This also includes material from the Dioceses of Carlisle and Durham.

A number of early bishops' registers have been published; these are listed here in chronological order:

[RAINE, JAMES, junior], ed. *The register, or rolls, of Walter Gray, Lord Archbishop of York, with appendices of illustrative documents.* Surtees Society **56**. 1872. For 1235-55.

[BROWN, WILLIAM], ed. *The register of Walter Giffard, Lord Archbishop of York, 1266-1279.* Surtees Society **109**. 1904.

[BROWN, WILLIAM], ed. *The register of William Wickwane, Lord Archbishop of York, 1279-1285.* Surtees Society **114**. 1907.

[BROWN, WILLIAM], ed. *The register of John le Romeyn, Lord Archbishop of York, 1289-1296.* 2 vols. Surtees Society **123** & **128**. 1913-17. Pt.2 also includes the register of Henry Newark, Archbishop of York, 1296-99.

[BROWN, WILLIAM], ed. *The register of Thomas of Corbridge, Lord Archbishop of York, 1300-1304.* Surtees Society **138** & **141**. 1925-28.

BROWN, WILLIAM, & THOMPSON, A. HAMILTON, eds. *The register of William Greenfield, Lord Archbishop of York, 1306-1315.* 2 vols. Surtees Society **145, 149,** & **151-3.** 1931-40.

HILL, ROSALIND M.T., et al, eds. *The register of William Melton, Archbishop of York, 1317-40.* Canterbury and York Society **70-71, 76** & **85.** 1977-97. v.1. Archdeaconry of Richmond; suffragans; spiritualities of Howden, Howdenshire, Allerton and Allertonshire. v.2. Archdeaconry of Cleveland, ed. David Robinson. v.3. Diverse Littere. v.4. Archdeaconry of Nottingham, ed. Reginald Brocklesby.

HILL, ROSALIND M.T. *The labourer in the vineyard: the visitations of Archbishop Melton in the Archdeaconry of Richmond.* Borthwick papers **35**. 1968. General discussion.

SMITH, DAVID M., ed. *A calendar of the register of Robert Waldby, Archbishop of York, 1397.* B.T.C. **2.** York: Bk.I.H.R., 1974.

SWANSON, R.N., ed. *A calendar of the register of Richard Scrope, Archbishop of York, 1398-1405.* B.T.C. **8** & **11.** York: Bk.I.H.R., 1981-5.

[THOMPSON, A. HAMILTON], ed. 'Documents relating to diocesan and provincial visitations from the registers of Henry Bowet, Lord Archbishop of York, 7 Oct. 1407-20 Oct. 1423, and John Kempe, Cardinal-Priest of Santa Balbina, Lord Archbishop of York, 20 July 1425-21 July 1452', in *Miscellanea vol. II.* Surtees Society **127.** 1916. Includes 'notes on canons of York and Beverley, and other clerks whose names occur ...'

BARKER, ERIC E., ed. *The register of Thomas Rotherham, Archbishop of York, 1480-1500.* Canterbury and York Society **69.** 1976. v.1. No more published.

PURVIS, J.S. 'The registers of Archbishops Lee and Holgate', *Journal of ecclesiastical history* **13**, 1962, 186-94. Brief discussion. 16th c.

A variety of other sources are also available. For a brief list of surviving visitation books see:

'Archiepiscopal visitations of the Dioceses of York and Chester', *Northern genealogist* **2**, 1896, 76-8.

Other works include (in rough chronological order):

SMITH, D.M. 'A reconstruction of the lost register of the vicars-general of Archbishop Thoresby of York', *B.I.B.* **3**, 1983-6. 29-61 & 102-13. Late 14th c.

SMITH, D.M. *Ecclesiastical cause papers at York: the court of York, 1301-1399.* B.T.C. **14.** York: Bk.I.H.R., 1988.

LONGLEY, KATHARINE M. *Ecclesiastical cause papers at York: Dean and Chapter's court, 1350-1843.* B.T.C. **6.** York: Bk.I.H.R., 1980.

'On some pardons or indulgences preserved in Yorkshire, 1412-1527', *Y.A.J.* **16**, 1900-1901, 369-423.

SHEILS, W.J. *Ecclesiastical cause papers at York: files transmitted on appeal, 1500-1883.* B.T.C. **9.** York: Bk.I.H.R. 1983. Including papers from the dioceses of Chester, Carlisle, Durham, and Sodor and Man, as well as York.

SKAIFE, ROBERT H. 'Extracts from the visitation books at York', *Y.A.J.* **15**, 1898-9, 224-41. 16-17th c. extracts from ecclesiastical records.

PAGE, WILLIAM, ed. *The certificates of the commissioners appointed to survey the chantries, guilds, hospitals, etc., in the County of York.* 2 vols. Surtees Society **91-2.** 1894-5. For 1546.

KITCHING, C.J. 'The chantries of the East Riding of Yorkshire, 1548', *Y.A.J.* **44,** 1972, 178-94. Includes names of incumbents in 1548.

PAGE, WILLIAM, ed. *The inventories of church goods for the counties of York, Durham, and Northumberland.* Surtees Society **97.** 1897. Transcripts, 1546-53.

'Visitations in the Diocese of York, holden by Archbishop Edward Lee', *Y.A.J.* **16,** 1900-1901, 424-58.

KITCHING, C.J., ed. *The royal visitation of 1559: act book for the Northern Province.* Surtees Society **187.** 1975.

SHEILS, W.J. *Archbishop Grindal's visitation, 1575: comperta et detecta book.* B.T.C. **4.** York: Bk.I.H.R., 1977.

'York High Commission causes and act books', *B.I.B.* **2,** 1979-82, 75-98. List, 16th c., with many names.

PURVIS, J.S. 'Dilapidations in parsonage property', *Y.A.J.* **36,** 1944-7, 316-37. Transcripts of 17th c. documents relating to repairs to parsonages *etc.,* includes names.

EVANS, PETER, ed. *Church fabric in the York Diocese 1613-1899: the records of the Archbishops' faculty jurisdiction.* B.T.C. **19.** 1995. York: Bk.I.H.R. Records of genealogical interest include such matter as pew allotments, placements and alterations of memorials, *etc.*

WHYTEHEAD, T.B. 'The discipline of the church', *Y.A.J.* **19,** 1906-7, 80-83. Transcript of selected penances ordered to be done, c.1730-31.

OLLARD, S.L., & WALKER, P.C., eds. *Archbishop Herring's visitation returns, 1743.* 5 vols. Y.A.S., R.S. **71, 72, 75, 77 & 79.** 1928-31. Replies to the Archbishop's queries, giving many names of clergy, churchwardens, etc. Includes appendices on Roman Catholics, dissenters, Archbishop Herring and his family, and clergy lists for York Minster, Southwell and Ripon.

ANNESLEY, CRESSIDA, & HOSKIN, PHILLIPA. *Archbishop Drummond's visitation returns, 1764.* B.T.C. **21.** York: Bk.I.H.R., 1997. To be completed; Yorkshire places A-G only in this volume. Much information on church life, mentions many names — especially clergy.

C. *Monastic Records*

Monastic foundations were an important feature of life in pre-Reformation Yorkshire, and works on their history and archives may contain useful information for the genealogist. A brief survey of these foundations is provided by:

LAWTON, GEORGE. *The religious houses of Yorkshire.* Simkin & Co., 1853.

See also:

BAILDON, WILLIAM PALEY, ed. *Notes on the religious and secular houses of Yorkshire, extracted from the public records.* 2 vols. Y.A.S., R.S. **17 & 81.** 1895-1931. Mainly from the *De Banco* rolls of the Court of Common Pleas, medieval.

PURVIS, J.S., ed. *Monastic Chancery proceedings (Yorkshire).* Y.A.S., R.S. **88.** 1934.

For nunneries, see:

BURTON, JANET E. *Yorkshire nunneries in the twelfth and thirteenth centuries.* Borthwick paper **56.** 1979. Not seen.

VICKERS, NOREEN. 'The social class of Yorkshire medieval nuns', *Y.A.J.* **67,** 1995, 127-32. Based on evidence from charters, archbishops' registers, wills, and heraldic visitations.

Cistercians

CLAY, C.T. 'The early abbots of the Yorkshire Cistercian houses', *Y.A.J.* **38,** 1955, 8-43. Biographical dictionary, to 1240.

FLETCHER, J.S. *The Cistercians in Yorkshire.* Society for Promoting Christian Knowledge, 1919.

Franciscans and Dominicans

GOLDTHORPE, L.M. 'The Franciscans and Dominicans in Yorkshire. Part 1. The Grey Friars', *Y.A.J.* **32,** 1936, 264-320 & 365-428. Includes lists of 'wardens of the Franciscan Convents', and 'Priors of the Dominican convents'.

Templars

MARTIN, E.J. 'The Templars in Yorkshire', *Y.A.J.* **29**, 1929, 366-85; **30**, 1931, 135-56. Includes 'A list of Templar lands in Yorkshire, 1185-1308'.

The Reformation

A number of works deal with monasteries during the Reformation period; most of these include many names of monks pensioned off.

CROSS, CLAIRE. 'Monasticism and society in the Diocese of York, 1520-1540', *Transactions of the Royal Historical Society* 5th series **38**, 1988, 131-45. Based on an analysis of bequests in wills.

CROSS, CLAIRE. *The end of medieval monasticism in the East Riding of Yorkshire.* E.Y.L.H.S. **47**. 1993. Includes 'pensions lists for the East Riding monasteries'.

CROSS, CLAIRE. 'The reconstitution of northern monastic communities in the reign of Mary Tudor', *N.H.* **29**, 1993, 200-204. Brief note.

FALLOW, T.M. 'Names of Yorkshire ex-religious, 1573: their pensions and subsidies to the Queen thereon', *Y.A.J.* **19**, 1906-7, 100-104.

CROSS, CLAIRE, & VICKERS, NOREEN. *Monks, friars and nuns in sixteenth century Yorkshire.* Y.A.S., R.S. **150**. 1995. Extensive listing, with many biographical notices.

CROSS, CLAIRE. 'A metamorphosis of ministry: former Yorkshire monks and friars in the sixteenth-century English protestant church', *Journal of the United Reformed Church Historical Society* **4**, 1989, 289-304. Identifies former monks and friars.

CLAY, JOHN WM., ed. *Yorkshire monasteries: suppression papers.* Y.A.S., R.S. **48**. 1912. Includes names of many monks granted pensions, and of purchasers of monastic property, *etc.*

D. The Clergy

The names of clergy may be found in most, if not all, of the works already cited. However, there are many works solely devoted to the identification of clergymen; these are listed here. A useful introduction to medieval sources is provided by:

SMITH, D.M. 'Sources for the medieval clergy of the York Diocese: a select bibliographical and archival guide', *B.I.B.* **3**, 1983-6, 127-40.

For a general discussion of an important source, see:

SMITH, DAVID M. 'The York institution act books: diocesan registration in the sixteenth century', *Archives* **13**(60), 1978, 171-9.

Senior clergy — Archbishops, deans, chancellors, precentors, archdeacons, prebendaries, *etc.*, — are listed in Le Neve's comprehensive and scholarly *Fasti* which has recently been completely revised:

LE NEVE, JOHN. *Fasti ecclesiae Anglicanae, 1300-1541. VI. Northern Province (York, Carlisle, and Durham),* comp. B. Jones. Athlone Press, 1963.

LE NEVE, JOHN. *Fasti ecclesiae Anglicanae, 1541-1857. IV. York Diocese,* comp. Joyce M. Horn & David M. Smith. Athlone Press, 1975.

For the Archbishops, see also:

DIXON, WILLIAM H. *Fasti Eboracenses: lives of the archbishops of York,* ed. James Raine. Longman, Green, Longman and Roberts, 1863.

HART, A. TINDAL. *Ebor: a history of the Archbishops of York from Paulinus to Maclagan, 627-1908.* York: William Sessions, 1986. Includes brief biographies.

Archdeacons are also listed in:

GILL, ARTHUR A.R. 'Archdeacons of the East Riding', *T.E.R.A.S.* **21**, 1915, 7-24. Includes biographical notes, 1130-1898.

CLAY, C.T. 'Notes on the early Archdeacons in the church of York', *Y.A.J.* **36**, 1944-7, 269-87 & 409-34. 12th c., biographical notes.

Early parochial clergy are comprehensively listed for a number of deaneries in:

THOMSON, A. HAMILTON, & CLAY, CHARLES TRAVIS, eds. *Fasti parochiales, vol.1[-2], being notes on the advowsons and pre-Reformation incumbents in the Deanery of Doncaster.* Y.A.S., R.S. **85** & **107**. 1933-43. To 1559.

LAWRANCE, N.A.H. *Fasti parochiales, vol. III. Deanery of Dickering.* Y.A.S., R.S. **129**. 1967. To 1662.

GURNEY, NORAH K.M., & CLAY, CHARLES, SIR. *Fasti parochiales, vol. IV, being notes on the advowsons and pre-Reformation incumbents of the parishes in the Deanery of Craven.* Y.A.S., R.S. **133**. 1971. To 1559.

LAWRANCE, N.A.H., ed. *Fasti parochialis, vol. V: Deanery of Buckrose.* Y.A.S., R.S. **143**. 1985. To 1660.

Other useful works on the clergy include (in rough chronological order):

GRIFFITH, L. 'Yorkshire clerics *temp.* Henry III', *Notes and queries* **153**, 1927, 24-5. List from assize rolls, 1245/6.

GRASSI, J.L. 'Royal clerks from the Archdiocese of York in the fourteenth century', *N.H.* **5**, 1970, 12-33. Includes 'list of the major York clerks'.

ROBINSON, DAVID. *Beneficed clergy in Cleveland and the East Riding, 1306-1340.* Borthwick papers **37**. 1969. General discussion.

BROWN, W. 'A list of benefices in the Diocese of York vacant between 1316 and 1319', in *Miscellanea* **1**. Y.A.S., R.S. **61**, 1920, 136-48. Includes many names of clergy.

MORAN, JO ANN HOEPPNER. 'Clerical recruitment in the Diocese of York, 1340-1530: data and commentary', *Journal of ecclesiastical history* **34**, 1983, 19-54. Based on ordination registers.

SMITH, D.M. 'A reconstruction of the York *sede vacante* register, 1352-1353', *B.I.B.* **1**, 1975-8, 75-90. Includes many institutions of clergy, *etc.*

MACKIE, PETER. 'Chaplains in the Diocese of York, 1480-1530: the testamentary evidence', *Y.A.J.* **58**, 1986, 123-33. Discussion of the evidence of wills.

[HENDERSON, W.G.,] ed. *Liber pontificalis Chr. Bainbridge, Archiepiscopi Eboracensis.* Surtees Society **61**. 1875. Includes ordination list, 1511.

MARSHALL, PETER. *The face of the pastoral ministry in the East Riding, 1525-1595.* Borthwick paper **88**. 1995. General discussion.

'The East Riding clergy in 1525-6', *Y.A.J.* **24**, 1917, 62-80. List of clergy and the value of their livings.

FALLOW, T.M. '[Yorkshire clergy taxed in 1526-7]', *Y.A.J.* **21**, 1910-11, 243-52.

ROBERTSHAW, WILFRID. 'A Yorkshire clergy list of the seventeenth century', *B.A.* **7**; N.S., **5**, 1933, 161-76. Muster roll, 1620s, of the York Diocesan clergy.

KAYE, WALTER J. 'Clergy subsidies in the Province of York, 1632, 1633 & 1634', *Y.A.J.* **31**, 1934, 157-69. Many clergy named.

BROWN, WILLIAM. 'Royalist clergy in Yorkshire 1642-5', in *Miscellanea* **1**. Y.A.S., R.S. **61**, 1920, 150-67. Petitions of clergy to the Earl of Newcastle, royalist commander in the north, from royalist clergy driven out of their livings by Parliamentary forces.

BROWN, W., ed. 'Presentations to livings in Yorkshire during the Commonwealth', in *Miscellanea* **1**. Y.A.S., R.S. **61**. 1920. 168-9. Brief.

COX, J. CHARLES. 'Parliamentary survey of the benefices of the East Riding', *T.E.R.A.S.* **2**, 1894, 24-67; **4**, 1896, 50-65. Names ministers.

SHEILS, W.J. *Restoration exhibit books and the northern clergy, 1662-1664.* B.T.C. **13**. York: Bk.I.H.R., 1987. Brief notes on clergy from the whole of the Province of York.

DALE, BRYAN. 'Ministers of parish churches in the West Riding during the Puritan Revolution', *B.A.* N.S. **1**, 1900, 431-41. Biographical notes on 41 Presbyterian clergymen who signed a declaration in 1648.

'Missing Yorkshire clergymen', *Y.N.Q.II.* **3**, 1907, 311-12. List of those not traced by *Crockfords* in 1907.

19th & 20th century clergy are listed in a number of diocesan year books:

Bradford Diocesan year book. Annual. 1933- .

The Ripon Diocesan calendar and church almanack ... Dewsbury: Joseph Ward, 1863-1922. Continued as: *The Ripon Diocesan handbook ...* Leeds: [ ], 1923-65. 1863 issue only seen.

Sheffield Diocesan calendar, clergy list, and churchman's handbook. Society for Promoting Christian Knowledge, 1915-39.

The York Diocesan calendar clergy list and church almanack ... Annual. York: John Sampson, 1862- . Title and publisher varies.

E. Local and Parochial

Many works on the church relate to particular places; these are listed here. Reference should also be made to the section on parish records (above, section 2), and to section 2 of *Information sources for Yorkshire genealogists* (volume 1 of *Yorkshire: the genealogists library guide*).

Aberford
'List of Aberford vicars', *Y.N.Q.II.* **5**, 1909, 154. 1230-1886.

Baildon
'Baildon notes, (1). An account of ye number of ye pews and seats in the chappell of Baildon and to whom they belong, 1723', *Y.N.Q.I.* **1**, 1888, 94-5.

Barningham
OLIVER, W. 'Our local parish clerks', *Teasdale Record Society* **14**, 1945, 8-13. With lists for Barningham, Brignall, Hutton Magna, Laithkirk, Romaldkirk and Startforth, 18-19th c.

Barnsley
TURNER, BENJAMIN. *St. George's church and schools, Barnsley: retrospect 1821 to 1912.* Barnsley: R.E. Griffiths, 1914. Includes many names of clergy, teachers, *etc.*

Beverley
The Minster
MCDERMID, RICHARD T.W., ed. *Beverley Minster fasti, being biographical notes on the provosts, prebendaries, officers and vicars in the church of Beverley prior to the dissolution.* Y.A.S., R.S. **149**. 1993.
LEACH, ARTHUR FRANCIS, ed. *Memorials of Beverley Minster: the chapter act book of the Collegiate church of S. John of Beverley, A.D. 1286-1347.* 2 vols. Surtees Society **98** & **108**. 1898-1903.
LEACH, ARTHUR F. 'A fifteenth-century fabric roll of Beverley Minster', *T.E.R.A.S.* **6**, 1898, 56-103; **7**, 1899, 50-83. Includes many names of tenants, *etc.*
Sanctuarium Dunelmense et sanctuarium Beverlacense. Surtees Society **[5.]** 1837. Includes register of 469 sanctuary seekers at Beverley, c.1478-1539. Described in:

THORNLEY, ISOBEL D. 'The sanctuary register of Beverley', *English historical review* **34**, 1919, 393-7. See also:
ELLIS, HENRY. 'An account of the register of persons who sought sanctuary at St. John of Beverley in Yorkshire, preserved among the Harleian manuscripts in the British Museum', *Archaeologia* **17**, 1814, 198-200. 15th c.

Black Friars
PALMER, C.F.R. 'The Friar Preachers, or Black Friars, of Beverley', *Y.A.J.* **7**, 1882, 32-43. Includes list of medieval burials, notes on benefactors, *etc.*

Bolton Abbey
THOMPSON, A. HAMILTON. *History and architectural description of the Priory of St. Mary, Bolton-in-Wharfedale, with some account of the Canons Regular of the order of St. Augustine and their houses in Yorkshire.* T.S. **30**. 1928.

Bowes
SAUNDERS, P.C. 'The Royal Free Chapel of Bowes', *Y.A.J.* **48**, 1976, 97-106. Discussion of a case heard in 1325 in the Archdeacon of Richmond's court; includes depositions of eight witnesses.

Bradford
TORRE, JOHN. 'List of vicars, rectors and testamentary burials in Bradford, from 1281 to 1667', *B.A.* N.S. **1**, 1900, 99-102.
'Bradford parish church vicars', *Y.N.Q.II.* **1**, 1905, 66. List, 1293-1896.
JUDSON, H.I. 'The early clergy of Bradford', *B.A.* **8**; N.S., **6**, 1940, 29-43. Medieval.
JUDSON, H.I. 'Notes on local clergy in Reformation times', *B.A.* **8**; N.S., **6**, 1940, 312-6. In Bradford, Kildwick and Skipton, *etc.*
'Ministers and churchwardens named in the Bradford Cathedral registers of the seventeenth century', *B.A.* **10**, N.S. **8**, 1962, 292.
DALE, BRYAN. 'Ministers of the parish church of Bradford and its three chapels during the Puritan Revolution', *B.A.* N.S., **2**, 1905, 124-34. Biographical notes.
DALE, BRYAN. 'Ministers of parish churches and chapels round about Bradford during the Puritan Revolution', *B.A.* N.S. **2**, 1905, 360-84. Mid-17th c., biographical notes.

SEWELL, AUGUSTUS BELL. 'A list of clerks in holy orders who have held the office of assistant stipendiary curate in the ancient parish church of Bradford', *B.A.* N.S. 3, 1912, 455-7.

KENZIE, K. 'Book presentation labels: collection no.1', 3, 1986, 12-15. Presentation labels, presumably from Sunday schools in the Bradford area, giving names of presentees.

Bridlington
SULLOWAY, J. 'The Austin canons of Bridlington', *Reports and papers of the Associated Architectural Societies* 33(1), 1915, 142-60. Includes list of priors, *etc.*

Brignall
See Barningham

Calverley
STAPLETON, HENRY. *Memorials of Calverley parish church and its forty-one vicars, with some account of the Old Hall, Calverley, Esholt Priory and Hall, and the daughter churches of Pudsey, Idle and Farsley.* Leeds: Richard Jackson, [1913?] Includes wills, list of seatholders at Idle, 1634, assessment 1695, monumental inscriptions, *etc.*

Clapham
WINSTONE, P.J. 'A history of the church in Clapham', *Journal* 9; N.Y.C.R.O.P. 29, 1982, 29-87. Includes lists of vicars, 12-20th c., churchwardens 1578-1976, and sextons 1747-1961.

Cottingham
WHITEHOUSE, JOHN. *The benefice of Cottingham: its parsons, patrons and property.* Cottingham Local History series 3. Cottingham: Cottingham Local History Society, 1973. Includes biographical notes on clergy.

Crambe
KIRK, GEO. E. 'Crambe church (N.R. Yorks)', *Y.A.J.* 25, 1920, 302-14. Includes list of vicars, medieval-17th c.

Dewsbury
CHADWICK, S.J. 'Notes on Dewsbury church and some of its rectors and vicars', *Y.A.J.* 20, 1908-9, 369-446. Includes wills.

HUNTER, JOSEPH. 'Dewsbury in the Archbishopric of York: its ecclesiastical history', *Collectanea topographica et genealogica* 1, 1834, 149-68.

Ecclesfield
See Handsworth

Eggleston Abbey
HODGSON, J.F. 'Eggleston Abbey', *Y.A.J.* 18, 1904-5, 129-82. Includes list of abbots.

Farnley
DAVEY, J. PETER. 'Mortuary', *Wh.N.* 27, 1998, 17. List of mortuaries paid in Farnley and Lindley, 1737-66.

Fishlake
FAIRBANK, F.R. 'The rectory of Fishlake', *Y.A.J.* 17, 1902-3, 413-9. Includes list of rectors, 13-14th c.

Fountains Abbey
COPPACK, GLYN. *English Heritage book of Fountains Abbey.* B.T. Batsford/ English Heritage, 1993. Includes list of abbots.

Giggleswick
BRAYSHAW, THOS. *Charters and other early documents relating to Giggleswick church.* Settle: Thos. Brayshaw, 1884.

BRAYSHAW, THOS. *Churchwardens of Giggleswick, 1638-1883.* Stackhouse: privately published, 1884.

'Vicarii de Giggleswick', *Y.N.Q.II.* 5, 1909, 182-3. List of vicars, 1190-1900.

Guisborough
See Selby Abbey

Handsworth
'Sale of presentations to a rectory and a vicarage', *T. Hunter A.S.* 2(1), 1920, 79-81. Handsworth and Ecclesfield, 1816.

Hornsea
HEATH, P. *Medieval clerical accounts.* St. Anthony's Hall publications 26. York: St. Anthony's Press, 1964. Includes transcripts of late 15th c. accounts for Hornsea.

Howden

BROWN, WILLIAM. 'The institution of the prebendal church at Howden', *Y.A.J.* **22**, 1913, 166-74. Includes list of rectors, 12-13th c.

WEDDALL, G.E. 'Churchwardens' accounts and other documents relating to Howden', *Y.A.J.* **19**, 1904-7, 455-81. Extracts, 16-17th c.

Huddersfield

JEPSON, DAVID. 'Have you checked all the registers for that baptism?' *H. & D.F.H.S.J.* 7(3), 1994, 92-3. List of places of worship from an 1881 Huddersfield directory.

Hull

CROSS, CLAIRE. *Urban magistrates and ministers: religion in Hull and Leeds from the Reformation to the Civil War.* Borthwick paper **67**. 1985. General study.

NEAVE, DAVID, et al. *Lost churches and chapels of Hull.* Hull: Hull City Museum & Art Galleries/Hutton Press, 1991. Gazetteer.

STUBLEY, PETER. *A house divided: evangelicals and the establishment in Hull, 1770-1914.* Hull: University of Hull Press, 1995. General study.

Hutton Magna
See Barningham

Illingworth

OAKLEY, G.R. *The story of Saint Mary's, Illingworth (1525-1925).* Halifax: F. King & Sons, 1924. Includes lists of clergy and various officers; also chapter on the Ramsden family, 16-20th c.

Kildwick
See Bradford

Kirk Ella

BICKFORD, J.A.R., & BICKFORD, M.E. *The rectors of Kirk Ella: the incumbents of the ancient parish of Elveley during the Middle Ages.* Kirk Ella: Kirk Ella Parish Magazine, 1990. Medieval; with biographical essays.

Kirkby Malzeard
See Masham

Kirklees Priory

CHADWICK, S.J. 'Kirklees Priory', *Y.A.J.* **16**, 1900-1901, 319-68. See also **17**, 1902-3, 420-33. Includes deeds, accounts, *etc.*

Kirkstall Abbey

BARNES, GUY D. *Kirkstall Abbey, 1147-1539: an historical study.* T.S. **58**. 1982. Includes list of abbots.

LONSDALE, ALLISTER. 'The last monks of Kirkstall Abbey', in *Thoresby miscellany* **15**. *T.S.* **53**, 1970, 201-15. Brief biographical notes on 29 monks.

'Kirkstall Abbey', *Y.N.Q.II.* **3**, 1907, 275-7. Includes list of abbots, 1147-1540.

'Kirkstall Abbey', *Northern genealogist* **2**, 1896, 118-9. List of benefactors.

Laithkirk
See Barningham

Leeds

THORESBY, RALPH. *Vicaria Leodiensis, or, the history of the church of Leedes, in Yorkshire, containing an account of the learned men, bishops and writers, who have been vicars of that populous parish, with the catalogues of their works, printed and manuscript ...* Joseph Smith, 1724.

'Thoresby's addenda and corrigenda to the Vicaria Leodiensis', in *Miscellanea* 1. *T.S.* **2**, 1891, 178-9.

RUSBY, JAMES. *St. Peter's at Leeds: being an account, historical and descriptive, of the parish church,* ed. James Gilliland Simpson. Leeds: Richard Jackson, 1896. Extensive; includes numerous monumental inscriptions, also biographical notes on vicars, lecturers and curates, list of churchwardens, list of 'testamentary burials', 15-17th c., *etc.*

'Notes on Leeds chapels', in *Miscellanea* [8]. *T.S.* **26**, 1924, 164-6. Brief note on chapel properties, including extracts from wills.

'The Vicarage of Leeds', in *Miscellanea* [8]. *T.S.* **26**, 1924, 166-8. Includes various names of trustees, 1697-1716.

WOOD, R.J. 'The return made by the Leeds commissioners to the Archbishop of York, in respect of the poor benefices in Leeds and the Bounty of Queen Anne', in *Miscellanea* **[8]**. *T.S.* **26**, 1924, 161-3.

CROSS, CLAIRE. 'The development of protestantism in Leeds and Hull, 1520-1640: the evidence from wills', *N.H.* **18**, 1982, 230-38.

YATES, NIGEL. *Leeds and the Oxford Movement: a study of high church activity in the rural deaneries of Allerton, Armley, Headingley and Whitkirk in the Diocese of Ripon.* T.S. **55**. 1975.

YATES, W.N. *The Oxford Movement and parish life: St. Saviour's, Leeds, 1839-1929.* Borthwick papers **48**. 1975.

See also Hull

Lightcliffe

MORGAN, F.L. 'Lightcliffe Chapel pew rent assessments', *T. Hal. A.S.* 1957, 69-71.

Lindley

See Farnley

Lockington

WALKER, P.C. 'The advowson of Lockington and some eighteenth century Chancery suits', *Y.A.J.* **26**, 1922, 189-229.

Marsden

BARRETT, A.R. *Some records of ye chapel of Marsden.* Huddersfield: Coates & Bairstow, 1910.

Marton Priory

PURVIS, J.S. 'Notes from the Diocesan Registry at York, ii: A visitation of Marton Priory in 1531', *Y.A.J.* **35**, 1942-3, 393-403.

Masham

CROSSLEY, E.W. 'Visitations of the Peculiar of Masham, 1741-1847', *Y.A.J.* **34**, 48-68. General discussion.

MCCALL, H.B. 'The peculiar of Masham cum Kirkby Malzeard', *Y.A.J.* **20**, 1908-9, 233-53. Includes list of clergy, 14-20th c.

Middleham

ATTHILL, WILLIAM, ed. *Documents relating to the foundation and antiquities of the Collegiate church of Middleham in the county of York, with an historical introduction, and incidental notices of the castle, town and neighbourhead.* Camden Society **38**. 1847. Includes lists of clergy, 16-19th c.

Middleton Tyas

'Middleton Tyas vicars', *Y.C.M.* **3**, 1893, 88-9. List, 1362-1890.

Mirfield

SHEILS, W.J. 'The deposited papers of the Mirfield fathers', *B.I.B.* **3**, 1983-6, 185-9. The Community of the Resurrection is an Anglican monastic community established in 1892.

Monk Bretton

WALKER, J.W. *An historical and architectural description of the Priory of St. Mary Magdalene of Monk Bretton in the West Riding of the County of Yorkshire.* Y.A.S. extra series **[5]**. 1926.

Mount Grace

BROWN, WM. 'History of Mount Grace', *Y.A.J.* **7**, 1882, 472-94. Includes pedigree of Lascelles, 17-18th c., notes on burials at the Priory, 15-16th c., list of priors, 14-16th c., and 8 deeds, 16-17th c.

Northallerton

SAYWELL, J.L. 'Northallerton church, Yorks', *Y.A.J.* **9**, 1886, 477-99. Includes list of clergy.

Pontefract Priory

CLAY, C.T. 'The early priors of Pontefract', *Y.A.J.* **38**, 1955, 456-64. Biographical notes, to mid-13th c.

HOLMES, RICHARD H.H. *The Black Friars of Pontefract: an account of their rise, progress and fall, with addenda comprising notes on the various subsequent owners of the property till it was restored to the church by Mr. Mortimer Fothergill in the early part of the eighteenth century.* [Pontefract]: T.W. Tew, [1891]. Includes notes on many bequests to the Priory (including 21 wills), with pedigrees of Austwick, 15-17th c., and Wilbore, 14-17th c.

Richmond

WENHAM, LESLIE P. 'The chantries, guilds, obits and lights of Richmond, Yorkshire', *Y.A.J.* **38**, 1955, 96-111, 185-214 & 310-32.

Richmond Archdeaconry

MCCALL, H.B. *Richmondshire churches.* Elliot Stock, 1910. Includes lists of clergy.

ADDY, JOHN. 'The archives of the Archdeaconry of Richmond', *Archives* 7(33), 1965, 25-33. Brief description.

'Diocesan registries: registry of Ripon (Archdeaconry of Richmond)', *Northern genealogist* **1**, 1895, 167-8. Brief calendar of documents.

THOMPSON, A. HAMILTON. 'The registers of the Archdeaconry of Richmond, 1361-1442', *Y.A.J.* **25**, 1920, 129-268. Transcript; includes 'biographical notes upon the more important clerks mentioned in the registers or notes'.

THOMPSON, A. HAMILTON. 'Some letters from the register of William Zouche, Archbishop of York', EDWARDS, J.G., GALBRAITH, V.H., & JACOB, E.F., eds. *Historical essays in honour of James Tait.* Manchester: 1933, 327-43. In Latin, relating to the Archdeaconry of Richmond, mid-14th c.

THOMPSON, A. HAMILTON. 'The register of the Archdeacons of Richmond, 1442-1477', *Y.A.J.* **30**, 1931, 1-132; **32**, 1937, 111-45. Includes list of incumbents of each parish in the period.

ESHELBY, H.D. 'The episcopal visitations of the Yorkshire Deaneries of the Archdeaconry of Richmond, in 1548 and 1554', *Y.A.J.* **14**, 1896-7, 390-421. Includes biographical notes on clergy, *etc.*

ADDY, JOHN. 'The Richmondshire apparitors', *Y.A.J.* **41**, 1966, 735-9. Brief discussion of an ecclesiastical court officer's duties.

CHADWICK, MICHAEL. 'Early churchwardens' presentments in the Archdeaconry of Richmond', *Y.A.J.* **40**, 1962, 657-61. Brief note, 16-17th c.

CHADWICK, MICHAEL. 'Richmondshire presentments of the reign of Queen Anne', *Y.A.J.* **40**, 1962, 371-7. Discussion of Archdeaconry of Richmond presentments.

BUTLER, L.A.S., ed. *The Archdeaconry of Richmond in the eighteenth century: Bishop Gastrell's 'Notitia': the Yorkshire parishes, 1714-1725.* Y.A.S., R.S. **146**. 1990. Parochial survey, based on returns made by the clergy, and giving details of patronage, clergy, schools, charities, *etc.*

Ripon

[FOWLER, J.T.], ed. *Acts of chapter of the Collegiate Church of Ss. Peter and Wilfrid, Ripon, A.D. 1452 to A.D. 1506.* Surtees Society **64**. 1875. Includes many wills.

[FOWLER, J.T., ed. *Memorials of the church of Ss. Peter and Wilfrid, Ripon.* 4 vols. Surtees Society **74, 78, 81** & **115**. 1882-1908. Includes transcripts of medieval chronicles, extracts from the bishops' registers, 1230-1538, list of clergy, c.1260-1886, accounts, fabric rolls, *etc.*, *ing.*

MORTIMER, JEAN E., ed. 'Ripon Minster fabric accounts 1661 to 1676', in WHITING, C.E., ed. *Miscellanea* **6**. Y.A.S., R.S. **118**, 1953, 85-150. Many names of tradesmen *etc.*

Romaldkirk

OLIVER, W. 'Rectors of Romaldkirk', *T.R.S.* **17**, 1946, 3-18. Biographical notices.

See also Barningham

Sallay Abbey

HARLAND, JOHN. *Historical account of the Cistercian abbey of Salley, in Craven, Yorkshire, founded 1147: its foundation and benefactors, abbots, possessions, compotus and dissolution, and its existing remains.* J. Russell Smith, 1853. Includes notes on abbots, deed abstracts, *etc.*

Sandal Magna

WALKER, J.W. 'Saint Helen's church, Sandal Magna', *Y.A.J.* **24**, 1917, 1-43. Includes list of vicars, 12-20th c., pedigree of Waterton of Walton, 13-18th c., notes on heraldry, *etc.*

Selby Abbey

DOBSON, BARRIE. 'The election of John Ousthorp as abbot of Selby in 1436', *Y.A.J.* **42**, 1971, 31-40. Includes list of electors.

HASLOP, G.S. 'A Selby kitchener's roll of the early fifteenth century', *Y.A.J.* **48**, 1976, 119-33. Accounts of Selby Abbey.
'Two fifteenth century lists of Yorkshire religious', *Y.A.J.* **29**, 1929, 386-9. Lists monks at Selby Abbey, 1436, and canons at Guisborough, 1425.

Sheffield

LAWRANCE, HENRY. 'The clergy in the neighbourhood of Sheffield at the time of the civil war', *T. Hunter A.S.* **4**, 1937, 69-84.

ODOM, W. *Fifty years of Sheffield church life, 1866-1916.* Home Words Office, 1917. Includes many biographical notes on clergy, *etc.*

ODOM, W. *Memorials of Sheffield and its churches.* Sheffield: J.W. Northend, 1922. Survey of many churches; includes brief notes on inscriptions.

WICKHAM, E.R. *Church and people in an industrial city.* Lutterworth Press, 1957. Few names, but an interesting general study of Sheffield church life, 19-20th c.

Skipton
See Bradford

South Crosland
'Extracts from a centenary souvenir of Holy Trinity church, South Crosland, 1829-1929', *H. & D.F.H.S.J.* **8**(3), 1995, 90. List of those connected with the church, with dates of death, 1870-1926.

Startforth
See Barningham

Tadcaster
KIRK, GEORGE E. *The parish church of St. Mary, Tadcaster, Yorkshire.* Leeds: J. Whitehead & Sons, 1939. Includes monumental inscriptions, notes on parish records, list of incumbents, *etc.*

Thornton
HOLGATE, IVY. 'Notes on records of Thornton Chapel', *B.A.* **10**; N.S. **8**, 1962, 255-72. Includes pew list, 1755.

Wakefield
WALKER, JOHN W. *The history of the old parish church of All Saints, Wakefield, now the cathedral church of the Diocese of Wakefield.* Wakefield: W.H. Milnes, 1888. Includes lists of clergy, monumental inscriptions, transcript of parish register 1600-1604 (with later extracts), *etc.*

WALKER, JOHN W. 'St. Mary's Chapel on Wakefield Bridge', *Y.A.J.* **11**, 1893, 146-68. Includes list of clergy, 1398-1535.

Wath
LUKIS, W.C. 'The church of Wath, near Ripon', *Reports and papers of the Associated Architectural Societies* **13**(1), 1875, 75-87. Includes list of rectors, with biographical notes; also notes on brasses, *etc.*

Weighton Deanery
See West Harthill Deanery

West Harthill Deanery
SMITH, M.E. 'A rural dean's visitation, 1843', *B.I.B.* **2**, 1979-82, 99-129. Returns for the Deanery of West Harthill or Weighton.

Whitkirk
KIRK, GEORGE E. *A history of the parish church of St. Mary, Whitkirk, Leeds.* Leeds: John Whitehead & Son, 1935. Includes monumental inscriptions, notes on clergy and the parish register, extracts from churchwardens' accounts, *etc.*

Whorlton
'Curates of Whorlton', *T.R.S.* **6**, 1941, 2-7. Biographical notes, 17-18th c.

Yarm
PALMER, C.F.R. 'The friar-preachers, or black friars, of Yarm', *Archaeological journal* **87**, 1880, 184-92. Includes biographical notes on some friars, list of burials, and notes on bequests to the Friary.

York
FALLOW, T.M., & HOPE, ROBERT CHARLES. 'The York church plate', *Y.A.J.* **8**, 1884, 300-48. Many names of clergy, benefactors, churchwardens, *etc.*
'York boy bishops', *Y.A.J.* **12**, 1893, 401-2. Includes list, 15-16th c.
PALLISER, D.M. *The Reformation in York, 1534-1553.* Borthwick papers **40**. 1971.

PALLISER, D.M. 'The unions of parishes at York, 1547-1586', *Y.A.J.* **46**, 1974, 87-102. Includes notes on closed churches.

ROYCE, EDWARD. *The Victorian church in York.* Borthwick paper **64**. 1983. Includes list of alterations in York parish boundaries, 1800-1974.

York Minster

AYLMER, G.E., & CANT, REGINALD, eds. *History of York Minster.* Oxford: Clarendon Press, 1977. Scholarly; includes a chapter on 'funeral monuments and the post-medieval sculpture'.

RILEY, HENRY THOMAS. 'York: the Dean and Chapter', in *First report of the Royal Commission on Historical Manuscripts.* H.M.S.O., 1874, 97. Brief survey.

CLAY, C.T. 'Notes on the chronology of the early deans of York', *Y.A.J.* **34**, 1939, 361-78. Notes on early medieval deans.

CLAY, C.T. 'The early precentors and chancellors of York', *Y.A.J.* **35**, 1943, 116-38. Biographical notes.

CLAY, C.T. 'The early treasurers of York', *Y.A.J.* **35**, 1943, 7-34. i.e. of the Minster.

HARRISON, FREDERICK. *Life in a medieval college: the story of the vicars-choral of York Minster.* John Murray, 1952. Many names.

[RAINE, JAMES, junior], ed. *The fabric rolls of York Minster, with an appendix of illustrative documents.* Surtees Society **35**. 1859. Extracts, Latin, c.1350-1639, with many names.

MILNER-WHITE, E. *Sixteenth century stained glass in York Minster and in the church of St. Michael le Belfrey.* St. Anthony's Hall publications **17**. St Anthony's Press, 1961.

PURVIS, J.S. 'A York account roll for A.D. 1537-1538', *Y.A.J.* **42**, 1971, 52-3. Lists many payments 'pro anima'.

CLAY, CHARLES TRAVIS, ed. *York Minster fasti, being notes on the dignitaries, archdeacons and prebendaries in the church of York prior to the year 1307.* 2 vols. Y.A.S., R.S. **123-4**. 1958-9.

DOBSON, B. 'The residentiary canons of York in the fifteenth century', *Journal of ecclesiastical history* **30**, 1979, 145-74. Includes list of 34 canons.

All Saints

KERRY, CHAS. 'History and antiquities of All Saints church, North Street, York', *Reports and papers of the Associated Architectural Societies* **9**(1), 1867, 57-69. Includes list of 18-19th c. rectors and medieval chantry chaplains, with notes on monuments, extracts from wills, *etc.*

Black Friars

PALMER, C.F.R. 'The Friar Preachers, or Black Friars, of York', *Y.A.J.* **6**, 1881, 396-419. Includes list of medieval burials, notes on benefactors, *etc.*

Holy Trinity Priory

SOLLOWAY, JOHN. *The alien Benedictines of York, being a complete history of Holy Trinity Priory, York.* Leeds: Richard Jackson, 1910. Extensive; includes lists of priors and incumbents.

STAPLETON, THOMAS. 'Historical details of the ancient religious community of secular canons in York prior to the Conquest of England, having the name of the church of the Holy Trinity, otherwise Christ Church, shewing its subsequent conversion into a Priory of Benedictine monks ... with biographical notes of the founder Ralph Paynell, and of his descendants, of whom William Paynell, his son, founded the Priory of Drax', in *Memoirs illustrative of the history and antiquities of the County and City of York communicated to the annual meeting of the Archaeological Institute of Great Britain and Ireland, held at York, July 1846 ...* John Murray, 1847. Includes much information on persons associated with the medieval priory.

St. Johns

CROSS, CLAIRE. 'The genesis of a Godly community: two York parishes, 1590-1640', in SHEILS, W.J., & WOOD, DIANA., eds. *Voluntary religion.* Studies in church history **23**. Oxford: Basil Blackwell for the Ecclesiastical History Society, 1986, 209-22. Study of the parishes of St. John's, Ousebridge, York, and All Saints, North Street, York, based on parish registers, churchwardens' accounts, and wills.

St. Martins
FRENCH, T.W. 'The advowson of St. Martin's church, York', *Y.A.J.* **40**, 1962, 496-505. Medieval.

St. Mary's Abbey
CRASTER, H.H.E., & THORNTON, M.E., eds. *The chronicle of St. Mary's Abbey, York, from Bodley ms. 39.* Surtees Society **148**. 1933. Includes lists of priors and monks.

SOLLOWAY, J. 'St. Mary's Abbey, York', *Reports and papers of the Associated Architectural Societies* **30**(1), 1909, 231-42. Includes list of abbots.

St. Sepulchre's Chapel
THOMPSON, A. HAMILTON. 'The chapel of St. Mary and the Holy Angels, otherwise known as St. Sepulchre's Chapel, at York', *Y.A.J.* **36**, 1944-7, 63-77 & 214-48. List of canons, with biographical notes, 12-16th c.

F. Nonconformity
The records of nonconformity provide much information of genealogical value, since a substantial proportion of the population attended nonconformist churches rather than the Church of England. Numerous publications relating to these churches are available; the works cited here are limited to those which are most likely to be of direct relevance to genealogists.

For a brief discussion of nonconformist records, see:

SHEILS, W.J. 'Sources for the history of dissent and Catholicism at the Borthwick Institute', *B.I.B.* **3**, 1983-6, 11-28.

Brief biographies of nonconformist ministers ejected from their livings at the Restoration are given in:

DALE, BRYAN. *Yorkshire puritanism and early nonconformity, illustrated by the lives of the ejected ministers, 1660 and 1662,* ed. T.G. Crippen. Bradford: Mr. Dale's literary executors, 1917.

Other general works on nonconformity include:

HEY, D.G. 'The pattern of nonconformity in South Yorkshire 1660-1851', *N.H.* **8**, 1973, 86-118. In the Deanery of Doncaster.

NEAVE, DAVID, & NEAVE, SUSAN. *East Riding chapels and meeting houses.* E.Y.L.H.S., 1990. Gazetteer of buildings, giving dates.

'Licensed meeting houses in the East Riding', *B.T.* **20**, 1984, 10-11. List, with names of persons who took out licences, including protestant dissenters and Roman catholics, 1708-1808.

ELLERBY, WILLIAM, & PRITCHETT, JAMES PIGOTT. *A history of the nonconformist churches of York,* ed. Edward Royle. B.T.C. **18**. York: Bk.I.H.R., 1993. General study; many names.

ROYLE, EDWARD. *Nonconformity in nineteenth-century York.* Borthwick paper **68**. 1985. General.

Baptists
SHIPLEY, C.E., ed. *The Baptists of Yorkshire, being the centenary memorial volume of the Yorkshire Baptist Association.* Bradford: William Byles & Sons, 1912. Provides brief histories of each church.

SELLERS, IAN, ed. *Our heritage: the Baptists of Yorkshire, Lancashire and Cheshire, 1647-1787-1887-1987.* Leeds: Yorkshire Baptist Association, 1987.

'Yorkshire Baptist congregations', *Y.C.M.* **3**, 1893, 72-4. List.

Bradford. Westgate
KENZIE, KENNETH. 'Bradford's emigrant Baptists', *Bod-kin* **3**(1), 1999, 17-20. Lists members of Westgate Baptist church from other places in 1839 and 1867.

Keighley
RHODES, JOSEPH. *A century of Keighley Baptist history.* Keighley: the Deacons, 1910. Includes list of persons in the church in 1830, and many other names.

Congregationalists/Independents
MIALL, JAMES G. *Congregationalism in Yorkshire: a chapter of modern church history.* John Snow & Co., 1868. Includes list of churches with names of ministers.

WHITEHEAD, THOS. *History of the Dales Congregational churches.* Keighley: Feather Bros., 1930. Histories of the individual churches, with many names.

Bradford
'Greenfield Congregational Church, Bradford', *Bod-kin* **3**, 1986, 8. Lists candidates for election to church management committee, 1896.

Hull

DALE, BRYAN. 'An old church roll', *Y.C.M.* **3**, 1893, 186-93. List of members of a Hull independent church, 1643-96, with names of pastors etc., to 1782.

Pudsey

RAYNER, SIMEON. 'A chapter in the ecclesiastical history of Pudsey', *B.A.* **1**, 1888, 124-31. History of the Congregational church; includes list of communicants 1713.

Sheffield. Upper Chapel

MANNING, J.E. *A history of Upper Chapel, Sheffield, founded 1662, built 1700, 'for the worship and service of Almighty God', with an appendix containing Timothy Jollie's register of baptisms.* Sheffield: Independent Press, 1900. The baptismal register is for 1681-1704. This was an independent chapel.

South Cave

TROUT, A.E. 'An old Yorkshire congregation: South Cave congregational church', *Transactions of the Congregational Historical Society* **11**, 1931, 174-88. Primarily biographical notes on ministers.

Friends

BESSE, JOSEPH. *Sufferings of early Quakers in Yorkshire, 1652-1690.* Facsimile of 1753 edition with new introduction by Michael Gandy. York: Sessions Book Trust, 1988.
'Yorkshire Quakers: the sufferings of Friends', *Old Yorkshire* **1**, 1881, 250-53. Many names, 17th c.
THISTLETHWAITE, W. PEARSON. *Yorkshire quarterly meeting (of the Society of Friends) 1665-1966.* Harrogate: the author, 1966. Extensive; many names.

Bradford

HODGSON, H.R. *The Society of Friends in Bradford: a record of 270 years. Also, a transcript of the Bradford registers 1650-1926, and notes on several meeting and burial places in the district.* Bradford: Percy Lund Humphries & Co., 1926.

Brighouse

CLAY, H. TRAVIS. 'Brighouse Quaker meeting', *T. Hal. A.S.* 1948, 19-25. Includes subscription list for new meeting house, 1744, and many other names.

Cleveland

HALL, DAVID S. 'Quakers in Cleveland', *C.T.L.H.S.B.* **6**, 1969, 3-9. Brief notes on each meeting.

Gildersome

'Trustees of Gildersome Meeting, 1796', *Cameo* 1993, no.2, 8-9. List of Quaker trustees.

Halifax

THISTLETHWAITE, PEARSON. 'Local Quakers and their meeting houses', *T. Hal. A.S.* 1986, 25-37. List of Halifax area meeting houses, with list and biographical notes on prominent Friends, 17-20th c.

Leeds

ALLOTT, WILFRID. 'Leeds Quaker meeting: a history based on the minute books of the Society of Friends in Leeds', in *The Thoresby miscellany* **14**. T.S. **50**, 1968, 1-77.
MORTIMER, JEAN, & MORTIMER, RUSSELL, eds. *Leeds Friends' minute book, 1692 to 1712.* Y.A.S., R.S. **139**. 1980. Includes a biographical dictionary of persons mentioned in the minute book. Important.
MORTIMER, JEAN E. 'Thoresby's poor deluded Quakers: the sufferings of Leeds Friends in the seventeenth century', in *Miscellany.* *T.S.* 2nd series **1**, 1990, 35-57.

Monk Bretton

ELLIOTT, BRIAN. 'The early Quakers of Monk Bretton, 1657-1700: a study of dissent in a South Yorkshire village', *T. Hunter A.S.* **10**(4), 1977, 260-72.

Rawdon

'Quaker meeting-house and Rawden, Yeadon, Idle and Keighley burial grounds', *Y.C.M.* **3**, 1893, 43-5. Abstracts of deeds.

Richmond

HALL, D.S. 'Quakers in Richmond and Swaledale', *C.T.L.H.S.B.* **20**, 1973, 1-11.

'Records of the Richmond monthly meeting of the Society of Friends', *North Riding Record Office report* 1966, 25-38. General discussion.

York

ALLOTT, STEPHEN. *Friends in York: the Quaker story in the life of a meeting.* York: William Sessions, 1978. Includes pedigrees of Tuke and Rowntree, 18-20th c.

SCOTT, DAVID. *Quakerism in York, 1650-1720.* Borthwick paper **80**. 1991. Includes various lists of Friends.

WRIGHT, SHEILA. *Friends in York: the dynamics of Quaker revival, 1780-1860.* Keele: Keele University Press, 1995. Includes various lists of names, and detailed bibliography.

WRIGHT, SHEILA. 'Quakerism and its implications for Quaker women: the women itinerant ministers of York Meeting, 1780-1840', in SHEILS, W.J., & WOOD, DIANA, eds. *Studies in church history* **27**. Oxford: Basil Blackwell for the Ecclesiastical History Society, 1990, 403-14.

Methodists

Wesley Historical Society (Yorkshire Branch) [newsletter]. 1962- . Includes news, brief articles, and regular lists of 'acquisitions' for the Society's library in Leeds.

'Methodist archives at the Borthwick Institute', *B.I.B.* **3**, 1983-6, 81-101. List.

Bradford. Kirkgate

DICKONS, J. NORTON. 'Kirkgate Chapel, Bradford, and its associations with Methodism', *B.A.* N.S., **2**, 1905, 68-97 & 205-24. Concerns 18th c. Methodism in Bradford generally; many names.

Holmfirth

MOORHOUSE, LINDA. 'Methodist parish magazines', *H. & D.F.H.S.J.* **7**(4), 1994, 115-7. Brief biographies of Holmfirth Methodists, 19th c.

Illingworth Moor

MOORE, HORACE. 'The story of Illingworth Moor Methodist Church', *T. Hal. A.S.* 1969, 29-54. Many names.

Normanby

TURNER, BERYL. 'Abstract of memorandum of the choice and appointment of new trustees of the United Methodist Free Church and premises situate at Normanby in the County of York', *J.Cl.F.H.S.* **6**(7), 1996, 45. List of trustees, 1884.

Sheffield. Norfolk Street

SEED, T. ALEXANDER. *Norfolk Street Wesleyan Chapel, Sheffield, being a history of this famous sanctuary, together with an account of the earlier and later history of Methodism in the town and neighbourhood.* Jarrold & Sons, 1907. Includes list of ministers, list of subscriptions received 1864-72, etc.

Sheffield. Surrey Street

NEWTON, S.C. 'The records of a Methodist Circuit: Surrey Street Chapel, Sheffield', *National Register of Archives South Yorkshire Committee bulletin* **3**, 1963, 11-14.

Stokesley Circuit

'Wesleyan preachers in the Stokesley Circuit, 1836-1837', *J.Cl.F.H.S.* **3**(12), 1988, 41. List.

Wetherby

'Wetherby Primitive Methodist Chapel trustees, 1872', *R.H.* **2**(5), 1994, 101.

Roman Catholics

BRADLEY, GEORGE T. 'The Leeds Diocesan archives', *Catholic archives* **2**, 1982, 46-51. Roman Catholic diocese; mainly personal papers of the bishops from 1688, but also includes family papers of Taylor of Cornsay House, Co. Durham.

AVELING, HUGH. *Northern Catholics: Catholic recusants of the North Riding of Yorkshire, 1558-1790.* Geoffrey Chapman, 1966. Includes a gazetteer of the incidence of recusancy with many names. Authoritative.

AVELING, HUGH. 'The Catholic recusants of the West Riding of Yorkshire, 1558-1790', *Proceedings of the Leeds Philosophical and Literary Society: Literary and Historical Section* **10**(6), 1963, 191-306. General study, with appendix listing names.

Short memoirs of the English martyrs, natives of Yorkshire (now forming the dioceses of Leeds and Middlesbrough) or who suffered in that county. Leeds: J. Whitehead and Son, 1885. Roman Catholic martyrs, 16-17th c.

AVELING, HUGH. *Post Reformation Catholicism in East Yorkshire, 1558-1790.* E.Y.L.H.S. **11**. 1960. General study; includes list of recusants, and of manuscript sources for Catholic history.

DICKENS, A.G. 'The first stages of Romanist recusancy in Yorkshire, 1560-1590', *Y.A.J.* **35**, 1941-2, 157-82. General study.

TYLER, P. *The ecclesiastical commission and Catholicism in the North, 1562-1577.* [ ], 1960. Useful discussion of the machinery used to keep Roman Catholicism in check.

AVELING, J.C.H. 'Catholic households in Yorkshire, 1580-1603', *N.H.* **16**, 1980, 85-101.

'A book of recusants', in TALBOT, CLARE, ed. *Miscellanea: recusant records.* C.R.S. **53**. 1961, 1-107. Lists of recusants, 1582 and 1595, mainly in the Province of York.

'Conformity in the North East, 1590-1625', *Catholic ancestor* **5**(6), 1995, 240-44. List of Catholic recusants who conformed, mainly from Yorkshire, from Exchequer records.

'Presentments of Papist recusants, 1597: the presentments of vicars, parsons, and curates against recusants', *Northern genealogist* **6**, 1903, 31-6. For the West Riding.

'West Riding presentments of recusants, 1597', in TALBOT, CLARE, ed. *Miscellanea: recusant records* C.R.S. **53**, 1960, 284-7.

'York Castle recusant lists', in TALBOT, CLARE, ed. *Miscellanea: recusant records* C.R.S. **53**, 1961, 276-9. For 1599, 1606 and 1619.

DICKENS, A.G. 'The extent and character of recusancy in Yorkshire, 1604', *Y.A.J.* **37**, 1951, 24-48. Includes list of the centres of Yorkshire recusancy, with names of Roman Catholic gentry.

DICKENS, A.G., & NEWTON, JOHN. 'Further light on the scope of Yorkshire recusancy in 1604', *Y.A.J.* **38**, 1955, 524-8.

PEACOCK, EDWARD. *A list of the Roman Catholics in the county of York in 1604.* J.C. Hotten, 1872.

AVELING, HUGH. 'The Catholic recusancy of the Yorkshire Fairfaxes, part. IV: Appendix: Chaplains to the Fairfax family', *Recusant history* **6**, 1961-2, 95-111. List, 17-18th c., with biographical notes.

'The northern book of compositions, 1629-32', in TALBOT, CLARE, ed. *Miscellanea: recusant records.* C.R.S. **53**, 1961, 307-437. Covers Yorkshire, Lancashire, and other northern counties.

BROWN, WILLIAM, ed. 'Subscriptions by recusants 1632-1639', in *Miscellanea* **1**. Y.A.S., R.S. **61**. 1920, 149. From the act book and subscription book of Archbishop Neile; brief list.

GERARD, JOHN, [ed.] 'Catholic chaplaincies and families in the North during the eighteenth century: notes and memoirs by Father John Laurenson, S.J., chaplain at Brough Hall, Yorkshire, 1808', in *Miscellanea* **4**. C.R.S. **4**. 1907, 247-59. Brief notes.

'Papist returns to the Archbishop of York in the 18th century', *Northern genealogist* **3**, 1900, 4-8, 84-91 & 177-80; **4**, 1901, 34-6. Selected returns from throughout Yorkshire, but especially Aberford, Leeds, Everingham, York, the Ainsty and the North Riding.

'Cosin's list of Catholics, non-jurors, &c., 1715', *Y.C.M.* **4**, 1894, 145-60.

TRAPPES-LOMAX, RICHARD, ed. 'Archbishop Blackburn's visitation returns of the Diocese of York, 1735', in *Miscellanea.* C.R.S. **32**, 1932, 204-388. Return of Papists.

JARRETT, BEDE. 'Rosary Confraternity lists', in *Miscellanea* **9**. C.R.S. **14**, 1914, 204-36. Includes names of boys at Bornhem College and girls at the school attached to Micklegate Bar Convent, York; also many names of Dominican fathers *etc.*

GILLOW, JOSEPH, ed. 'The Huddleston obituaries', in *Miscellanea* **1**. C.R.S. **1**, 1905, 123-33. Anniversaries noted by Dom John Huddleston whilst chaplain to the Preston and Ingleby families, including some for Yorkshire.

WORRAL, E.S., ed. *Return of papists, 1767: Diocese of Chester.* Occasional publications **1**. C.R.S., 1980. The diocese included the Richmond Archdeaconry.

PERKINS, JOHN P., & LITTON, PAULINE M. *Roman Catholics in North West Yorkshire, covering the Deaneries of Boroughbridge, Catterick, Richmond, & parts of Lonsdale, extracted from returns of papist, 1767: Diocese of Chester.* Harrogate: the authors, 1990.

'Some dissenters and their meeting places in Hull and the East Riding', *B.T.* **20**, 1984, 10. List of Roman Catholics who took the oath, 1778.

SUPPLE-GREEN, JENNIFER FRANCES. 'The Catholic revival in Yorkshire, 1850-1900', *Leeds Philosophical and Literary Society, Literary and Historical Section proceedings* **21**(3), 1990, 203-95. Scholarly study.

SUPPLE, JENNIFER F. 'The role of the Catholic laity in Yorkshire, 1850-1900', *Recusant history* **18**, 1987, 304-17. General discussion.

SUPPLE, JENNIFER F. 'The Catholic clergy of Yorkshire, 1850-1900: a profile', *N.H.* **21**, 1985, 212-35.

Agbrigg

VARLEY, JUDITH. 'A list of Agbrigg Catholics in the County of York', *H. & D.F.H.S.J.* **10**(1), 1996, 23-4. Brief.

Egton

SHEILS, W.J. 'Catholics and their neighbours in a rural community: Egton chapelry, 1590-1780', *N.H.* **34**, 1998, 109-33. Includes table of 'the eighteenth-century Catholic community', giving surnames.

Everingham

HANSOM, JOSEPH S., ed. 'Everingham papists, 1767', in *Miscellanea* **6**. C.R.S. **7**. 1909. 257-9. Reprinted from the *Northern genealogist* **3**, 1900, 6-8. From a return made to the Archbishop of York.

Grosmont Priory

BODDY, G.W. 'Catholic missioners at Grosmont Priory', *Journal* **4**; N.Y.C.R.O.P. **10**, 1976, 65-76.

Holderness

BLASHILL, THOMAS. 'Some certificates as to recusants in Holderness', *Journal of the British Archaeological Association* N.S. **3**, 1897, 275-80.

Hull

HIRST, JOSEPH HENRY. *The blockhouses of Kingston-upon-Hull and who went there: a glimpse of Catholic life in the penal times, and a missing page in local history.* 3rd ed. A. Brown & Sons, 1913. The 'blockhouses' were prisons; includes much information on 16th c. Catholic martyrs.

MCCLELLAND, MARIA G. 'The first Hull Mercy nuns: nineteenth-century case study', *Recusant history* **22**, 1994, 199-221.

MCCLELLAND, MARIA. 'In search of the Hull Mercy nuns: an archival travelogue', *Catholic archives* **16**, 1996, 37-52. Account of research methods.

Masham

HANSOM, J.S., ed. 'Recusants of Masham, Yorkshire', in *Miscellanea* **3**. C.R.S. **3**, 1906, 82-6. From the act books of Masham peculiar court, 1589-1628.

Middlesbrough Diocese

CONNELLY, ROLAND. *No greater love: the martyrs of the Middlesbrough Diocese.* Great Wakering: McCrimmon, 1987. Brief biographies of 29 Catholic martyrs, 16-17th c.

York

AVELING, J.C.H. *Catholic recusancy in the city of York, 1558-1791.* C.R.S. publications (monograph series) **2**. 1970. Includes extensive genealogical notes on 'York citizen, papist families, 1688-1791'.

THOMAS, PHILLIP. 'The Privy Council and vagrant runagate priests in Elizabethan York', *Y.A.J.* **69**, 1997, 173-92. Discussion of the activities of Roman Catholic priests, late 16th c.

HANSOM, J.S., ed. 'Papist returns for the City of York and part of the Ainsty 1735', in *Miscellanea* 4. C.R.S. 4. 1907, 368-73.

COLERIDGE, H.J. *St. Mary's Convent, Micklegate Bar, York (1686-1887).* Burns and Oates, 1887. Includes many biographical notes on Roman Catholic nuns.

GREGORY, M., SISTER. 'The 17th and 18th century archives of the Bar Convent, York', *Catholic archives* 10, 1990, 3-7. Institute of the Blessed Virgin Mary; brief description.

HANSOM, J.S. 'The nuns of the Institute of Mary at York from 1677 to 1825', in *Miscellanea* 4. C.R.S. 4. 1907, 353-67. Biographical notes on 81 nuns.

O'BRIEN, SUSAN. 'Women of the English Catholic community: nuns and pupils at the Bar Convent, York, 1680-1790', in LOADES, JUDITH, ed. *Monastic studies: the continuity of tradition.* Bangor: Headstart, 1990, 267-82. General discussion.

F. *Jews*

Leeds

FREEDMAN, MURRAY. *1891 census Leeds: list of Jewish residents.* Leeds: Murray Freedman, 1994.

KRAUSZ, ERNEST. *Leeds Jewry: its history and social structure.* Cambridge: W. Heffer and Sons for the Jewish Historical Society of England, 1964. General study.

Sheffield

KRAUSZ, ARMIN. *Sheffield Jewry: commentary on a community.* Ramat-Gan: Bar Ilan University, 1980. Many names.

York

DAVIES, ROBERT. 'The medieval Jews of York', *Y.A.J.* 3, 1875, 147-97. General study.

DOBSON, R.B. *The Jews of medieval York and the massacre of March 1190.* Borthwick papers 45. 1974.

DOBSON, R.B. 'The decline and expulsion of the medieval Jews of York', *Transactions of the Jewish Historical Society of England* 26, 1979, 34-52. General discussion. Includes names of purchasers of Jewish property.

4. ESTATE RECORDS

The records of estate administration constitute a mine of information for the genealogist. Deeds, leases, surveys, rentals, accounts, *etc.*, are all capable of yeilding much valuable genealogical information. For Yorkshire, a considerable number of books and journal articles on this subject are available, and are listed here.

A. *Guides to Records.*

A variety of lists and calendars of records in particular institutions are available. In addition to those mentioned below, reference should be made to the works cited in section 2 of *Information sources for Yorkshire genealogists* (vol.2 of *Yorkshire: the genealogists library guide*).

Manorial records at the Borthwick Institute are listed in:

BURG, JUDITH. 'Manorial records at the Borthwick Institute', *B.I.B.* 4(1), 1987, 6-15. List.

See also:

WEBB, C.C. 'Sources for the history of houses at the Borthwick Institute', *B.I.B.* 3, 1983-6, 168-84. Orientated towards houses rather than their occupiers, but may nevertheless be useful to the genealogist.

Deeds Registers

From the 18th century, many deeds were registered in the deeds registries of the three ridings. A number of works on these registries are available:

SHEPPARD, FRANCIS & BELCHER, VICTOR. 'The deeds registries of Yorkshire and Middlesex', *Journal of the Society of Archivists* 6, 1980, 274-86.

TATE, W.E. 'The five English district statutory registries of deeds', *Bulletin of the Institute of Historical Research* 20, 1943-45, 97-105. The ridings of Yorkshire accounted for 3 of the 5 registers.

BODDINGTON, C.A. *The East Riding Register of Deeds: a guide for users.* Rev. ed. Beverley: East Riding of Yorkshire Archive Office, 1995. Brief pamphlet.

NUSSEY, J.T.M. 'The West Riding Registry of Deeds', *Y.A.S., F.H.P.S.S.N.* 55, 1979, 70-72.

TURNER, MARGARET. 'Registered deeds as a source for family historians', *Cameo* 1992, no. 1, 7-9. Discussion of the West Riding Deeds Registry.

ARCHER, C.A., & WILKINSON, R.K. 'The Yorkshire registries of deeds as sources of historical dates on housing markets', *Urban history yearbook* 1977, 40-47.

SHEPPARD, FRANCIS, BELCHER, VICTOR, & COTTEREL, PHILIP. 'The Middlesex and Yorkshire deeds registries and the study of building fluctuations', *London journal* **5**, 1979, 176-217. Based on a count of registrations.

Enclosure Awards

Enclosure awards provide many names of individuals with interests in the properties enclosed. For Yorkshire, awards are listed in:

ENGLISH, BARBARA. *Yorkshire enclosure awards.* Studies in regional and local history **5**. Hull: University of Hull, 1985. See also:

NEAVE, VANESSA. *Handlist of East Riding enclosure awards.* Beverley: Attic Press, 1971.

On enclosures, see also:

LEADAM, I.S. 'The inquisition of 1517: enclosures and evictions ... part II', *Transactions of the Royal Historical Society* N.S., **7**, 1893, 127-292. Gives names of many landowners in Norfolk, Yorkshire, Herefordshire, Staffordshire and Hampshire.

A number of published local records of enclosure are listed in section 4H below.

B. *Domesday Book and other Surveys*

Domesday book, written in 1086, is the earliest general survey of landowners in England, and the earliest record likely to be of interest to present-day genealogists. A number of editions are avalable; the most convenient is:

FAULL, MARGARET L., & STINSON, MARIE, eds. *Domesday book 30: Yorkshire.* 2 vols. Chichester: Phillimore & Co., 1986. See also:

ELLIS, ALFRED S. 'Biographical notes on the Yorkshire tenants named in Domesday book', *Y.A.J.* **4**, 1877, 114-57, 214-48 & 384-415; **5**, 1879, 289-330.

Other county-wide surveys include:

RUSBY, JAMES. 'Yorkshire nobility, 1189', *Y.C.M.* **1**, 1891, 341-2. List of tenants in chief.

'Humberston's survey', *Y.A.J.* **17**, 1902-3, 129-53. Of estates held by attainted rebels in 1569.

WILLAN, T.S. 'The Parliamentary surveys for the North Riding of Yorkshire', *Y.A.J.* **31**, 1934, 224-89. Discussion of an important survey of 1649.

C. *Deeds and Charters*

Numerous calendars of deeds and charters are available for Yorkshire. Ten volumes of the Yorkshire Archaeological Society's record series have been devoted to *Yorkshire deeds;* these volumes are of a miscellaneous character, and are all worth checking for particular names.

BROWN, WILLIAM, ed. *Yorkshire deeds.* Y.A.S., R.S. **39**. 1909. From various collections.

BROWN, WILLIAM, ed. *Yorkshire deeds, vol. II.* Y.A.S., R.S. **50**. 1914. From various collections.

BROWN, WILLIAM, ed. *Yorkshire deeds vol. III.* Y.A.S., R.S. **63**. 1922. English abstracts from various collections.

CLAY, CHARLES TRAVIS, ed. *Yorkshire deeds vol. IV.* Y.A.S., R.S. **65**. 1924. From various collections.

CLAY, CHARLES TRAVIS, ed. *Yorkshire deeds vol. V.* Y.A.S., **69**. 1926. English abstracts of deeds in various collections; includes index of places in vols 1-5, and notes on the families of Habton and Stockeld.

CLAY, CHARLES TRAVIS, ed. *Yorkshire deeds, vol. VI.* Y.A.S., R.S. **76**. 1930. English abstracts; includes notes on Neville and Sewerby families, an index to Yorkshire deeds in the *Descriptive catalogue of ancient deeds in the Public Record Office,* and corrigenda to previous volumes.

CLAY, CHARLES TRAVIS, ed. *Yorkshire deeds, vol. VII.* Y.A.S., R.S. **83**. 1932. English abstracts, from various collections.

CLAY, CHARLES TRAVIS, ed. *Yorkshire deeds, vol. VIII.* Y.A.S., R.S. **102**. 1940. English abstracts, from various collections.

HEBDITCH, M.J., ed. *Yorkshire deeds, vol. IX.* Y.A.S., R.S. **111**. 1948. From miscellaneous collections.

STANLEY PRICE, M.J., ed. *Yorkshire deeds, vol. X.* Y.A.S., R.S., **120.** 1955. From miscellaneous collections.

A collection of deeds now held at Sheffield Archives is calendared in:
HALL, THOMAS WALTER. *Catalogue of the charters, deeds and manuscripts in the Public Reference Library at Sheffield.* Sheffield: J.W. Northend, 1912.

A bookseller's collection of Yorkshire deeds is abstracted in:
'The value of old parchment documents in genealogical and topographical research', *Genealogical quarterly* **4,** 1935-6, 71-87.

Miscellaneous abstracts may be found in:
BAIN, JOSEPH. 'Notes on a collection of eight early documents relating to Yorkshire ...', *Archaeological journal* **36,** 1879, 272-6. Miscellaneous medieval deeds.
SYKES, WILLIAM. 'Royal grants in Yorkshire 1684 to 1700', *Y.A.J.* **10,** 1889, 309-12. Deed abstracts.
'Local muniments', *Y.A.J.* **3,** 1877, 161-9. Various medieval deeds.
See also:
N[ICHOLS], J.G. 'Charges made by Christopher Lascelles gent., against Sir Robert Riche, Chancellor of the Court of Augmentations, for malversations in granting leases of church lands in Yorkshire and Northumberland', *Topographer & Genealogist* **2,** 1853, 285-7.

Antiquaries Collections

Many major collections of deeds have been collected by antiquaries; these are listed here.

Bosville

HALL, THOMAS WALTER. *Yorkshire: a descriptive catalogue of land-charters and court-rolls from the Bosvill & the Lindsay collections; Waldershelf manor and the Knights Hospitallers of Jerusalem; the Park in the City of Sheffield; ancient charters and instruments of Ughill, Waldershelf & Norton Lees near Sheffield.* Sheffield: J.W. Northend, 1930.

Burton

'Yorkshire deeds', *Y.A.J.* **16,** 1900-1901, 84-107; **17,** 1902-3, 96-126. Medieval-17th c.; from the collections of Dr Burton and Marmaduke Tunstall.

Constable

ELLIS, A.S. 'Yorkshire deeds', *Y.A.J.* **12,** 1893, 92-115, 230-62 & 289-308; **13,** 1895, 44-76. Abstracts of a collection of deeds made by William Constable.

Jackson

HALL, T. WALTER, & THOMAS, A. HERMANN. *Descriptive catalogue of the charters, rolls, deeds, pedigrees, pamphlets, newspapers, monumental inscriptions, maps and miscellaneous papers forming the Jackson collection at the Sheffield Public Reference Library.* Sheffield: J.W. Northend, 1914. Mainly concerned with Yorkshire, but also includes material from nine other counties.

Lindsay

HALL, THOMAS WALTER. *Yorkshire charters from the Lindsay collection: translations and notes.* Sheffield: J.W. Northend, 1928.
See also Bosville

Phillips

FAWTIER, ROBERT. 'Hand-lists of charters and deeds in the possession of the John Rylands Library, IV: the Phillips charters', *Bulletin of the John Rylands Library, Manchester.* **9,** 1925, 248-85. Lists numerous deeds from various places in Derbyshire, Yorkshire, Kent, *etc.*

Tunstall

See Burton

Wheat

HALL, THOMAS WALTER. *Descriptive catalogue of charters, copy court rolls, and deeds forming part of the Wheat collection at the Public Reference Library, Sheffield; also others from private collections, with abstracts of Sheffield wills proved at York from 1560 to 1566 and 285 genealogies deduced therefrom.* Sheffield: J.W. Northend, 1920.

Wilson
HUNTER, JOSEPH. 'Prefatory letter to Wilson's Yorkshire deeds', *Y.A.J.* **4**, 1877, 64-8.

Early Yorkshire Charters

For genealogical research in the 12th century and earlier, the starting point in Yorkshire must be this massive work begun by William Farrer and completed by Sir Charles Clay. These are listed here together, although most of them deal with the records of particular fees and could equally well be listed in the section below.

FARRER, WILLIAM, ed. *Early Yorkshire charters, being a collection of documents anterior to the thirteenth century made from the public records, monastic chartularies, Roger Dodsworth's manuscripts, and other available sources.* 3 vols. Edinburgh: Ballantyne Hanson & Co., 1914. 644 deeds, 10-12th c.

CLAY, CHARLES TRAVIS, & CLAY, EDITH MARGARET. *Early Yorkshire charters vols I-III ... a consolidated index of persons and places.* Y.A.S., R.S. Extra series IV. 1942. Index to Farrer's work.

CLAY, CHARLES TRAVIS, ed. *Early Yorkshire charters vol IV-[V]. The Honour of Richmond, based on the manuscripts of the late William Farrer.* Y.A.S., R.S. Extra series 1-2. 1935-6. Includes medieval pedigrees of the lords of the honour, and of Manfield and Lascelles. Officials of the Honour are listed in the second part.

CLAY, CHARLES TRAVIS, SIR, ed. *Early Yorkshire charters vol. VI. The Paynel fee, based on the manuscripts of the late William Farrer.* Y.A.S., R.S. Extra series 3. 1939. Includes pedigrees of Paynel, 12-14th c. (folded) and Stonegrave, 12-13th c.

Early Yorkshire charters vol. VII. The Honour of Skipton, based on the manuscripts of the late William Farrer. Y.A.S., R.S. Extra series 5. 1947. Includes notes on the early constables of Skipton, and priors of Bolton Abbey, with medieval pedigrees of the lords of the honour, and also of Mauleverer of Beamsley, Vavasour and Rilston.

Early Yorkshire charters vol. VIII. The Honour of Warenne. Y.A.S., R.S. Extra series 6. 1949. Includes pedigrees of Warenne and Neufmarche.

CLAY, CHARLES TRAVIS, ed. *Early Yorkshire charters, Vol IX: The Stuteville fee, based on the manuscripts of the late William Farrer.* Y.A.S., R.S. extra series 7. 1952. Includes Stuteville pedigrees, folded, 12-13th c., also pedigree of Boltby, 12-13th c.

CLAY, CHARLES TRAVIS, ed. *Early Yorkshire charters, vol. X. The Trussebut fee, with some charters of the Ros fee, based on the manuscripts of the late William Farrer.* Y.A.S., R.S. Extra series 8. 1955. Includes Trussebut pedigree, 12-13th c.

CLAY, CHARLES TRAVIS, ed. *Early Yorkshire charters, vol XI. The Percy fee. Based on the manuscripts of the late William Farrer.* Y.A.S., R.S. Extra series 9. 1963. Includes Percy pedigrees, 11-14th c., also Darel pedigree, 12-13th c.

CLAY, CHARLES TRAVIS, SIR, ed. *Early Yorkshire charters, vol. XII. The Tison fee, based on the manuscripts of the late William Farrer.* Y.A.S., R.S. Extra series 10. 1965. Includes medieval pedigrees of Tison, Salvain of Thorpe Salvain, and Constable of Flamborough (folded).

Feet of Fines

The curiously named 'feet of fines' constitute an important and extensive series of deeds, enrolled in the records of the Court of Common Pleas. Many have been published by the Yorkshire Archaeological Society in its record series; there is also one Surtees Society volume, and a few *Yorkshire archaeological journal* articles.

CLAY, CHARLES, SIR. 'Yorkshire final concords of the reign of Henry II', *Y.A.J.* **40**, 1962, 78-89.

[BROWN, W.,] ed. *Pedes finium Ebor regnante Johanne, A.D. MCXCIX — A.D. MCCXIV.* Surtees Society 94. 1897.

BROWN, WILLIAM. 'Pedes finium Ebor., tempore Ricardi Primi', *Y.A.J.* **11**, 1891, 174-88.

PARKER, JOHN, ed. *Feet of fines for the County of York from 1218 to 1231.* Y.A.S., R.S. 62. 1921.

PARKER, JOHN. ed. *Feet of fines for the County of York from 1232 to 1246.* Y.A.S., R.S. **67**. 1925.

PARKER, JOHN, ed. *Feet of fines for the County of York from 1246 to 1272.* Y.A.S., R.S. **82**. 1932.

SLINGSBY, F.H., ed. *Feet of fines for the County of York from 1272 to 1300.* Y.A.S., R.S. **121**. 1956.

ROPER, M., ed. *Feet of fines for the county of York from 1300 to 1314.* Y.A.S., R.S. **127**. 1965.

BAILDON, W. PALEY, ed. *Feet of fines for the County of York from 1327 to 1347, 1-20 Edward III.* Y.A.S., R.S. **42**. 1910.

BAILDON, W. PALEY, ed. *Feet of fines for the County of York, from 1347 to 1377, 21-51 Edward III.* Y.A.S., R.S. **52**. 1915.

COLLINS, FRANCIS, ed. *Feet of fines for the Tudor period.* Y.A.S., R.S. **2, 5, 7 & 8**. 1887-1908.

BRIGG, WILLIAM, ed. *Yorkshire fines for the Stuart period.* Y.A.S., R.S. **53 & 58**. 1915-17. Contents: v. 1. 1603-1614. v. 2. 1614-1625.

D. *Private Estates*

The larger proprietors in Yorkshire — and some of the smaller ones as well — had estates in various parts of the county, and sometimes in other counties as well. The estate papers of a number of families have been listed and published; these and other works on private estates are listed here — although works dealing with only a few places are listed topographically in sub-section F below.

Allan

'The Havelock-Allan archive', *North Riding Record Office report* 1972, 23-46. Discussion of an 18th c. estate archive, with a summary list of the records of the Allan family.

Armytage

BICKLEY, FRANCIS B., ed. *A catalogue of the muniments at Kirklees, in the West Riding of the County of York, from the time of King Richard I to the end of the eighteenth century, in the possession of Sir George John Armytage.* Privately printed, 1900. Abstracts of 857 deeds relating to the West Riding.

Beaumont

WARD, J.T. 'The Beaumont family's estates in the nineteenth century', *Bulletin of the Institute of Historical Research* **35**, 1962, 169-77. Brief discussion.

Bolling

TEMPEST, ARTHUR, MRS. 'The Bollings of Wadlans, Calverley, &c.', *Y.G.* **2**, 1890, 231-4. See also 278-9. Deed abstracts relating to the family, 15-16th c.

Bosville

'Bosville deeds', *Y.A.J.* **13**, 1895, 219-25. 14-16th c. deeds.

Boynton

COLLIER, C.V. 'Documents at Burton Agnes', *T.E.R.A.S.* **18**, 1912, 56-114; **19**, 1913, 1-39. Abstracts of 287 deeds relating to property in numerous places.

Bradfer-Lawrence

HOYLE, R.W. 'Archival notes: the Bradfer Lawrence collection', *Y.A.J.* **51**, 1979, 163-7. Brief description of a major collection of estate papers at the Yorkshire Archaeological Society, including those of Lister of Gisburne, Lambert of Calton, and Wilson of Eshton; also miscellaneous documents relating to Craven, Fountains Abbey, *etc., etc.*

WENTWORTH, GEORGE. 'Deeds relating to property in various parts of Yorkshire, from the muniment room at Woolley Park, near Wakefield', *Archaeological journal* **18**, 1861, 60-65. Medieval.

Burgh

PERCEVAL, CHARLES SPENCER. 'Notes on a selection of ancient charters, letters and other documents from the muniment-room of Sir John Lawson of Brough Hall, near Catterick in Richmondshire, Baronet', *Archaeologia* **47**, 1883, 179-204. Title deeds, *etc.,* of Burgh family, medieval.

Cholmley

'The Cholmleys of Whitby', *North Riding Record Office report* 1970, 5-14. Discussion of estate archives.

Clifford

SCOTT, DANIEL. 'Recent discoveries in the muniment rooms of Appleby Castle and Skipton Castle', *Transactions of the Cumberland and Westmorland Antiquarian and Archeaological Society* N.S., **18**, 1918, 189-210. Discussion of the Clifford family's muniments.

Constable

COLLIER, C.V. 'Documents at Everingham', *T.E.R.A.S.* **22**, 1919, 1-31. Abstracts of 114 deeds, 13-17th c., mainly of the Paynell and Poucher families, in the archives of the Constable family.
See also Stapleton

Crompton

'The Wood End records', *North Riding Record Office report* 1970, 15-20. Crompton family archives, mainly relating to Thornton le Street, Thornton le Moor, South Otterington, Newsham, and Thornton le Beans, 16-19th c.

Crowe

JACQUES, HUGH. 'The Kiplin Hall archive', *Journal* **5**; N.Y.C.R.O.P. **13**, 1977, 59-78. General discussion and summary of estate papers of the Crowe family relating to Bolton on Swale, Catterick, Ellerton on Swale, Kiplin, Scorton and Tunstall, 16-20th c.

Dawnay

PERRY, JENNIFER. 'The Dawnay archive', *Journal* **4**; N.Y.C.R.O.P. **10**, 1976, 93-110. Relating to estates in Danby, Wykeham, Baldersby, Sessay, Cowick and Snaith, 14-19th c.

De La Pole

FRYDE, E.B. *The wool accounts of William De La Pole*. St. Anthonys Hall publications **25**. York: St. Anthony's Press, 1964. Not seen.

Devonshire, Earls of

FOWKES, D.V., & POTTER, G.R., eds. *William Senior's survey of the estates of the first and second Earls of Devonshire, c. 1600-1628*. Derbyshire Record Society, **13**. 1988. The estate included property in Yorkshire.

Dundas

See Zetland

Fairbanks

A guide to the Fairbank collection of maps, plans and surveyors' books and correspondence in the Reference Library. Sheffield: Sheffield City Libraries, 1936. Description of the business archive of a firm of surveyors, which includes numerous plans and field books naming land owners, *etc.,* 18-19th c. See also:
HALL, THOMAS WALTER. *The Fairbanks of Sheffield 1688-1848.* Sheffield: N.W. Northend, 1932. Facsimiles of surveys from the Fairbank collections: includes the names of some landowners. Also includes brief pedigree of Fairbanks, 18-19th c.
'The Fairbank collection', *T. Hunter A.S.* **4**, 1937, 172-4.

Fairfax

CONNOR, W.J. 'The Fairfax archives: a study in dispersal', *Archives* **11**, 1973-4, 76-85. Discussion of the way in which an estate archive has been dispersed.

Fitz Peter

HOLMES, RICHARD. 'The charter-history of a long life: Adam Fitz Peter of Birkin', in *Miscellanea* [3]. *T.S.* **9**, 1899, 56-61. Calendar of deeds, 12th c.

Fortibus

DENHOLM YOUNG, N. 'The Yorkshire estates of Isabella de Fortibus', *Y.A.J.* **31**, 1934, 389-420. 13th c. General discussion.

Halifax, Earls of

See Wood

Ingilby

HORWOOD, ALFRED J. 'The manuscripts of Sir Henry Ingilby, Bart., of Ripley Castle, Co.York', in *Sixth report of the Royal Commission on Historical Manuscripts, Part I. Report and appendix.* H.M.S.O., 1877, 352-95. Includes calendar of documents from Fountains Abbey and Bridlington Priory. Few other estate records, but many letters.

Ingram

BICKLEY, FRANCIS L. 'The manuscripts of the Hon.Frederic Lindley Wood preserved at Temple Newsam, Leeds', in HISTORICAL MANUSCRIPTS COMMISSION. *Report on manuscripts in various collections, vol.VIII.* H.M.S.O., 1913, 1-195. Deeds and letters of the Ingram family, 17-18th c., etc.

Lacy

LYONS, PONSONBY, ed. *'Compoti* of the Yorkshire estates of Henry de Lacy, Earl of Lincoln', *Y.A.J.* **8**, 1884, 351-8. 1294-5.

Langdale

'Genealogia antiquæ familiæ Langdalorum', *Y.A.J.* **11**, 1891, 372-431. Abstracts of Langdale family deeds, 14-17th c., includes folded pedigree.
See also Stapleton

Lumley

BEASTALL, T.W. *A North Country estate: the Lumleys and Saundersons as landowners, 1600-1900.* Chichester: Phillimore, 1975. Includes pedigree of the Lumley-Saunderson connection. The estate included property in Co. Durham, Yorkshire (especially Sandbeck) and Lincolnshire (especially Fillingham).

Meaux

BICKLEY, FRANCIS. *Report on the manuscripts of the late Reginald Rawdon Hastings, vol.I.* Historical Manuscripts Commission, 1928. Includes medieval deeds of Melsa or Meaux family of Sutton in Holderness.

Mowbray

GREENWAY, D.E., ed. *Charters of the Honour of Mowbray, 1107-1191.* Records of social and economic history, N.S., **1.** Oxford University Press for the British Academy, 1971. Includes pedigrees of Aubigny and Mowbray, 11-12th c.

Norfolk, Dukes of

MEREDITH, ROSAMUND, ed. *Catalogue of the Arundel Castle manuscripts, being the muniments of His Grace the Duke of Norfolk, Earl Marshal, K.G., relating to the Yorkshire, Nottingham and Derbyshire estates of the Dukes of Norfolk and their predecessors, with an appendix consisting of a calendar of Talbot letters, part of the Bacon Frank collection.* Sheffield: Sheffield City Council Libraries and Arts Committee, 1972.

Paynall

See Constable

Percy

M[ARTIN], M.T., ed. *The Percy chartulary.* Surtees Society **117.** 1911. Includes over 110 medieval deeds, half of them of Yorkshire interest, and 25% from Northumberland.

Poole

E., A. 'A schedule of deeds belonging to James Poole, esq', *T.R.S.* **16,** 1946, 11-13. For properties at Barnard Castle, Sledwick, Barningham and Bowes, 17-18th c. (held at the Yorkshire Archaeological Society).

Poucher

See Constable

Pudsay

LITTLEDALE, RALPH PUDSAY, ed. *The Pudsay deeds: the Pudsays of Bolton and Barforth and their predecessors in those manors.* Y.A.S., R.S. **56.** 1916. Includes folded pedigrees of Bolton, 13-14th c., Pudsay, 14-17th c., Berford, Cleseby, Hudleston and Laton, 12-14th c.

Ripon, Marquis of

HORWOOD, ALFRED J. 'The manuscripts of the Most Honourable the Marquis of Ripon at Studley Royal, Co.York', in *Sixth report of the Historical Manuscripts Commission. Part 1. Report and appendix.* H.M.S.O., 1877, 243-50. Includes brief calendar of 'Fountains Abbey deeds and documents'; also lists much material on genealogy and heraldry.

St Quinton

COLLIER, C.V. 'Documents at Scampston', *T.E.R.A.S.* **21,** 1915, 25-69. 139 deeds, 14-15th c., relating to the St. Quinton estates.

Saunderson
See Lumley

Scarbrough, Earls of
BEASTALL, T.W. 'A South Yorkshire estate in the late nineteenth century', *Agricultural history review* **14**, 1966, 40-44. Brief note on the estate of the Earl of Scarbrough.

Scrope
'The Scropes of Danby', *North Riding Record Office report* 1969, 9-24. Discussion of estate archives.

Stapleton
WILLIAMS, J. ANTHONY. 'Catholic family papers in Hull University library', *Catholic archives* **3**, 1983, 27-31 & 37. Brief discussion of the estate papers of Stapleton of Carlton, Langdale of Holme and Houghton, Constable of Everingham, *etc.*

Talbot
See also Norfolk, Dukes of

Travis
'The Travis trust and the 400 acres', *Don. Anc.* 6(1), 1993, 12-16; 6(2), 1993, 32-4. Lists tenants, 18-20th

Wandesford
M'CALL, HARDY BERTRAM. *Story of the family of Wandesford, of Kirklington & Castlecomer, compiled from original sources, with a calendar of historical manuscripts.* Simpkin Marshall Hamilton Kent & Co., 1904. Castlecomer is in Co. Kilkenny. The appendix calendars 269 deeds, mainly relating to Yorkshire.

Wentworth
COOPER, J.P., ed. *Wentworth papers, 1597-1628.* Camden 4th series **12**. Royal Historical Society, 1973.
'The manuscripts of Mrs.Wentworth of Woolley Park, Yorkshire', in HISTORICAL MANUSCRIPTS COMMISSION. *Report on manuscripts in various collections, vol.II.* H.M.S.O., 1903, 367-432. Wentworth family letters and papers, mainly 17-18th c.

Wharncliffe
HORWOOD, ALFRED J. 'The manuscripts of the Right Honourable Lord Wharncliffe', in *Third report of the Royal Commission on Historical Manuscripts.* H.M.S.O., 1872, 224-6. List of estate papers, medieval-18th c.

Wilson, John, & Sons
'A collection of business papers from eighteenth century Leeds', *Business History Society bulletin* **12**(5), 1938, 76. Brief note on the papers of John Wilson & Sons, of Leeds, linen drapers, 18th c.

Winn
'The Nostell papers: the archives of the Winn family ...', *Bulletin of the National Register of Archives* **10**, 1959, 1722.

Wood
SMITH, D.M. 'The archives of the Earl of Halifax', *B.I.B.* **2**, 1979-82, 141-54. Wood family; the papers listed mainly include family letters, diaries, and papers relating to Garrowby and East Riding estates.

Wyvill
'The Wyvill of Constable Burton family archive', *North Riding Record Office report* 1967, 35-43.

Yarburgh
SWANSON, R.N. 'The Yarburgh muniments', *B.I.B.* **2**, 1979-82, 212-25. Brief list of estate papers relating to Heslington, Fulford, Snaith, Cowick, *etc., etc.,* medieval-20th c.

Zetland
'The Zetland (Dundas) archive', *North Riding Record Office report* 1971, 13-48. Includes summary list of a North Riding estate archive.

E. *Ecclesiastical Estates and Chartularies, etc.*
In the medieval period, a great deal of property was owned by ecclesiastical institutions such as churches, monasteries, dioceses, *etc.* Their records had a much greater chance of survival than the records of private families, since they were 'perpetual' institutions. Monastic deeds and charters were frequently collected together into chartularies, many of which have been published. These publications, together with a variety of other works relating to ecclesiastical estates, are listed here.

Arthington Nunnery
LANCASTER, W.T. 'Four early charters of Arthington Nunnery', in *Miscellanea* **[6]**. *T.S.* **22**, 1915, 118-28. Medieval.

Bolton Abbey

Bolton Abbey was technically a priory; however, it is commonly referred to as an Abbey. This is reflected in the titles below.

KERSHAW, IAN, ed. *Bolton Priory rentals and ministers accounts, 1473-1539.* Y.A.S., R.S. **132**. 1970.

KERSHAW, IAN. *Bolton Priory: the economy of a northern monastery.* Oxford: Oxford University Press, 1973. Study of a medieval monastic estate.

HOYLE, RICHARD. 'Monastic leasing before the dissolution: the evidence of Bolton Priory and Fountains Abbey', *Y.A.J.* **61**, 1989, 11-37. Includes many unpublished leases *etc.,* additional to those edited elsewhere.

Bridlington Priory

LANCASTER, WILLIAM T., ed. *Abstracts of the charters and other documents contained in the chartulary of the Priory of Bridlington in the East Riding of the County of York.* Leeds: [J. Whitehead & Son], 1912.

PURVIS, J. S., ed. 'A selection of monastic rentals and disclosure papers', in *Miscellanea* 3. Y.A.S., R.S. **80**. 1931, 1-148 & 207-22. Chiefly relating to Bridlington Priory.

See also Byland Abbey

Byland Abbey

A[LDRIDGE], H.R. 'Yorkshire charters', *British Museum quarterly* **7**, 1932-3, 118-9. Brief note on charters from Byland Abbey; also from Bridlington Priory and Newburgh Priory.

M[ILLAR], E.G. 'Byland Abbey charters', *British Museum quarterly* **7**, 1933, 39-40. Brief description.

See also York

Easby Abbey

WENHAM, L.P. 'The dissolution of St. Agatha's Abbey, Easby, 1536', *Journal* **8**; N.Y.C.R.O.P., **27**, 1981, 33-64.

Esholt Priory

BAILDON, W. PALEY. 'Esholt Priory estate accounts, 1539-1540', *B.A.* **6**; N.S., **4**, 1921, 27-32.

Fountains Abbey

LANCASTER, WILLIAM T., ed. *Abstracts of the charters and other documents contained in the chartulary of the Cistercian Abbey of Fountains in the West Riding of the County of York.* 2 vols. Leeds: J.Whitehead & Son, 1915.

WALBRAN, JOHN RICHARD, ed. *Memorials of the Abbey of St. Mary of Fountains.* Surtees Society **42**. 1863. Includes 91 documents, the most extensive of which is a 'valor' of its lands at the dissolution.

WALBRAN, J.R., & RAINE, JAMES, junior, eds. *Memorials of the abbey of St. Mary of Fountains ... vol.II, part 1.* Surtees Society **67**. 1878. Not completed. Includes 'A genealogical and biographical memoir of the Lords of Studley in Yorkshire (with the descent of the Abbey of Fountains to the present time)', which was originally published separately, Ripon: William Harrison, 1841.

FOWLER, J.T., ed. *Memorials of the abbey of St. Mary of Fountains ... vol III, consisting of bursar's books, 1456-1459, and memorandum book of Thomas Swynton 1466-1458.* Surtees Society **130**. 1918.

KILLICK, H.F. 'Some notes on the chartulary of Fountains Abbey', *B.A.* **6**; N.S., **4**, 1921, 303-21. General discussion.

B[ELL], H. I. 'A register of Fountains Abbey', *British Museum quarterly* **7**, 1932-3, 16-18. Brief description.

MICHELMORE, D.J.H., ed. *The Fountains Abbey lease book.* Y.A.S., R.S. **140**. 1981.

MICHELMORE, D.J.H., ed. *The Fountains Abbey rental, 1495/6.* Leeds: the editor, 1974.

See also Bolton Priory

Gisburn Priory

[BROWN, WILLIAM], ed. *Cartularium Prioratus de Gyseburne, Ebor. Diceseos, ordinis S. Augustini, fundati A.D. MCXIX.* 2 vols. Surtees Society **86** & **89**. 1899-94. Includes rent roll, c. 1300.

Grandmont Priory

E., H. 'Survey of Grandmont Priory, in Yorkshire', *Collectanea topographica et genealogica* **2**, 1835, 365-7. 16th c.

Haltemprice Priory

COX, J. CHARLES. 'The Priory of Haltemprice', *T.E.R.A.S.* **18**, 1912, 12-26. Mainly concerning its land acquisitions; includes list of priors.

Healaugh Priory

PURVIS, J.S., ed. *The chartulary of the Augustinian Priory of St. John the Evangelist of the Park of Healaugh.* Y.A.S., R.S. **92**. 1936.

Kirkstall Abbey

LANCASTER, W.T., & BAILDON, W. PALEY, eds. *The coucher book of the Cistercian Abbey of Kirkstall in the West Riding of the County of York.* T.S. **8**. 1904.

STANSFELD, JOHN. 'Rent-roll of Kirkstall Abbey', in *Miscellanea.* **1**. *T.S.* **2**. 1891, 1-21. For 1459; includes list of Abbey charters in the British Library.

'Ancient deeds', *Y.C.M.* **1**, 1891, 88-94, 129-40 & 228-38; **2**, 1892, 105-16; **3**, 1893, 76-88; **4**, 1894, 117-24. From Kirkstall Abbey, medieval.

'The possession of Kirkstall Abbey in Leeds', *Miscellanea.* **[2]**. *T.S.* **4**, 1895, 37-41 & 81-116. Survey, c.1539-41, with names of tenants.

Knights Hospitallers

CROSSLEY, E.W., ed. 'The Preceptories of the Knights Hospitallers', in *Miscellanea* **4**. Y.A.S., R.S. **94**, 1937, 71-174 & 190-213. Includes ministers' accounts, court rolls, etc., medieval-17th c.

Lenton Priory

BURTON, J.E. 'A roll of charters for Lenton Priory', *B.I.B.* **2**, 1979-82, 13-26.

Lewes Priory, Sussex

CLAY, C.T. 'The Yorkshire portion of the Lewes chartulary', *Y.A.J.* **31**, 1934, 290-319.

Malton Priory

GRAHAM, ROSE. 'The finance of Malton Priory 1244-57', in her *English ecclesiastical studies: being some essays in research in medieval history.* S.P.C.K., 1929, 247-70. Reprinted from *Transactions of the Royal Historical Society* N.S., **18**, 1904, 131-56.

Marrigg Priory

S., T. 'Ground plan and charters of St. Andrews Priory in the parish of Marrigg', *Collectanea topographica et genealogica* **5**, 1838, 100-124, 157-60 & 221-59. Latin abstracts; also includes list of prioresses, 1250-1530, and pedigrees of Powlett, 17-18th c., and Uvedale, 16th c.

Meaux Abbey

EARLE, ALBERT. *Essays upon the history of Meaux Abbey, and some principles of mediaeval land tenure, based upon a consideration of the Latin chronicles of Meaux (A.D. 1150-1400).* A. Brown & Sons, 1906. Includes biographical notes on abbots but primarily of interest for the abbey estates.

M. 'Extracts from the chronicles or cartulary of the abbey of Meaux, Co. York, containing the genealogies of Scurres, Hyldehard and Stutevylle', *Collectanea topographica et genealogica* **1**, 1834, 9-13. Includes list of benefactors buried at Meaux.

Monk Bretton Priory

WALKER, J.W., ed. *Abstracts of the chartularies of the Priory of Monkbretton.* Y.A.S., R.S. **66**. 1924.

PURVIS, J.S. 'New light on the chartularies of Monkbretton Priory', *Y.A.J.* **37**, 1951, 67-71. Brief note.

Newburgh Priory

See Byland Abbey

Newland Preceptory

CROSSLEY, E.W., ed. 'The Preceptory of Newland', in *Miscellanea* **1**. Y.A.S., R.S. **61**, 1920, 1-83. Includes accounts, 1539-40, charters, 13th c., 'inventories of evidences', and 1628 rentals of Batley and Hellifield in Craven.

Nostell Priory

LANCASTER, W.T., ed. 'A fifteenth century rental of Nostell Priory', in *Miscellanea* **1**. Y.A.S., R.S. **61**. 1920, 108-35. For 1578.

RANSOME, GWENLLIAN C., ed. 'The chartulary of Tockwith alias Scokirk, a cell to the Priory of Nostell', *Miscellanea* **3**. Y.A.S., R.S. **80**, 1931, 149-206 & 223-7.

Pontefract Priory

HOLMES, RICHARD, ed. *The chartulary of St. John of Pontefract, from the original document in the possession of Godfrey Wentworth, esq., of Woolley Park.* Y.A.S., R.S. **25 & 30**. 1899-1902. Includes many pedigrees.

Rievaulx Abbey

[ATKINSON, J.C.], ed. *Cartularium abbathiae de Rievalle, ordinis Cisterciensis, fundatae anno MCXXXII.* Surtees Society **83**. 1899.

Roche Abbey

AVELING, JAMES H. *The history of Roche Abbey, from its foundation to its dissolution.* John Russell Smith, 1870. Includes many extracts from deeds and notes on its estate.

ADDY, SIDNEY OLDALL. *Cartae xvi Abbatium Rupensem spectantes: XVI charters of Roche Abbey.* Sheffield: Leader and Sons, 1878.

ADDY, SIDNEY OLDALL. 'Roche Abbey charters: transcripts with introduction & notes', ed. T. Walter Hall. *T. Hunter A.S.* **4**, 1937, 226-48.

Sallay Abbey

MCNULTY, JOSEPH, ed. *The chartulary of the Cistercian Abbey of St. Mary of Sallay in Craven.* 2 vols. Y.A.S., R.S. **87 & 90**. 1933-4. Indcludes biographical notes on abbots.

Selby Abbey

MCDONNELL, K.G.T. 'The archives of Selby Abbey', *Y.A.J.* **44**, 1972, 170-72. Brief discussion.

FOWLER, J.T., ed. *The concher book of Selby.* Y.A.S., R.S. **10 & 13**. 1891-3.

TILLOTSON, JOHN H., ed. *Monastery and society in the late middle ages: selected account rolls from Selby Abbey, Yorkshire, 1398-1537.* Woodbridge: Boydell & Brewer, 1987.

'Account roll of Selby Abbey', *Y.A.J.* **15**, 1898-9, 408-19.

HOLT, BERYL, ed. 'Two obedientiary rolls of Selby Abbey', in WHITING, C.E., ed. *Miscellanea* **6**. Y.A.S., R.S. **118**. 1953, 31-52. Accounts.

Swine Priory

DUCKETT, GEORGE, SIR. 'Charters of the Priory of Swine in Holderness', *Y.A.J.* **6**, 1881, 113-24.

Whitby Abbey

ATKINSON, J.C., ed. *Cartularium abbathiae de Whiteby, ordinis S. Benedict.* 2 vols. Surtees Society **69 & 72**. 1879-81.

York
Saint Leonards Hospital

GREENWAY, DIANA E. 'A lost cartulary of St. Leonards Hospital, York', *Y.A.J.* **42**, 1971, 178-80. Brief note.

RAGG, FREDERICK W. 'Charters to St. Peter's (St. Leonard's) Hospital, York, and to Byland Abbey', *Transactions of the Cumberland and Westmorland Antiquarian & Archaeological Society* N.S., **9**, 1909, 236-70. Includes pedigrees, 12-13th c.

York Minster

BISHOP, T.A.M., ed. 'Extents of the Prebends of York [c. 1295]', in *Miscellanea* **4**. Y.A.S., R.S. **94**. 1937, 1-38 & 175-89.

BURTON, JANET E., ed. *The cartulary of the treasurer of York Minster and related documents.* B.T.C. **5**. York: B.I.H.R., 1978.

York Diocese

GENTLES, I.J., & SHEILS, W.J. *Confiscation and restoration: the Archbishopric estates and the civil war.* Borthwick papers **59**. 1981. Includes lists of tenants *etc.*

G. *Tithe Records and Maps*

The right of the clergy to claim tithes was a major source of their income until the nineteenth century, and generated a vast amount of documentation. For a general discussion, see:

SHEILS, W.J. 'The right of the church: the clergy, tithe, and the courts at York, 1540-1640', in SHEILS, W.J., & WOOD, DIANA, eds. *The church and wealth.* Studies in church history, **24**. Oxford: Basil Blackwell, 1987, 231-55.

The commutation of tithes in the nineteenth century involved the compilation of maps naming landowners and occupiers. For Yorkshire, these maps and the associated apportionments are listed in:

FONGE, C.R. *Tithe awards and maps at the Borthwick Institute: a handlist.* List and index 11. York: Borthwick Institute, 1994.

For some earlier tithe records, see:

PURVIS, J.S., ed. *Select 16th century causes in tithe from York Diocesan Registry.* Y.A.S., R.S. 114. 1949.

Local Tithe Records

Bainbridge

ROBERTS, FRED, & ROBERTS, JOYCE. *The township of Bainbridge in the middle of the nineteenth century: the census enumerators' schedules for 1841 & 1851, & the tithe apportionment & map, 1844.* N.Y.C.R.O.P. 21. 1979.

Bradford

JONES, BRIAN. *Bradford tithe returns, 1638.* Bradford: Brian Jones, 1995.

Great Ayton, *etc.*

MARCHANT, JOSEPHINE, & MARCHANT, ALAN. *Tithe maps of Great Ayton, Little Ayton, Tunstall, Marton, Hinderwell.* Yarm on Tees: Christian Inheritance Trust, 1996.

Halifax

OXLEY, J.E. 'Tithe rental of Halifax parish', *T. Hal. A.S.* 1934, 77-114. List of those liable to pay tithes, 16th c.

Hutton

MARCHANT, JOSEPHINE, & MARCHANT, ALAN. *Tithe maps of Hutton Fields, Hutton village, Middleton-on-Leven, Skutterskelf, Sexhow, Crathorne, Hilton; estate maps, Rudby.* Yarm on Tees: Christian Inheritance Trust, 1993.

Leeds

LUMB, G.D. 'Lease, dated 1687, of the tithe of hay in Leeds, by the Earl of Burlington to Thomas Dixon', in *Miscellanea 7. T.S.* 24, 1919, 401-19. Includes list of tithe payers.

SPENCE, RICHARD T. 'Tithes and tithe-holders in the parish of Leeds from the dissolution to the restoration', in *Miscellany* 19. T.S. 63, 1990, 1-26. Includes list (folded) of 'Leeds parish tithes and tenants, 1579-1675'.

Muker

BOUSTED, M.J., ed. *Upper Swaledale education and society: documents to illustrate the history of Muker and Keld & its schools in the 19th & early 20th century.* N.Y.C.R.O.P. 48. 1992. Includes tithe apportionment, 1841 and 1845.

Saddleworth

H., J.M. 'Saddleworth tithes in 1669', *B.S.H.S.* 14(2), 1984, 20-5. Lists tithepayers.

Sessay

'Tithes', *J.Cl.F.H.S.* 5(7), 1993, 39-42. Lists tithe payers for Sessay, 1743 and 1773.

Settle

HILL, AUDREY M., ed. *Settle in the middle of the nineteenth century: the tithe apportionment 1844; the census returns 1851.* N.Y.C.R.O.P. 14. 1977.

Thornaby on Tees

MARCHANT, JOSEPHINE, & MARCHANT, ALAN. *Tithe map of Thornaby-on-Tees in the parish of Stainton.* Yarm on Tees: Christian Inheritance Trust, 1996.

H. *Local Estate Records*

Many estate records relating to particular places have been published. Those publications which are devoted solely to one or two places are listed here; publications which have a broader remit are listed in the appropriate places above.

Acomb

RICHARDSON, HAROLD., ed. *Court rolls of the manor of Acomb.* 2 vols. Y.A.S., R.S. 131 & 137. 1969-78. For 1544-1846.

Adel

LANCASTER, W.T. 'Adel', in *Miscellanea* [2]. *T.S.* 4, 1895, 261-86. Includes deeds extracts, abbreviated survey of the manor of Cookridge 1540, list of tenants 1460, *etc.*

Airedale

'Survey of the River Aire from Leeds to Weeland', in *Miscellanea* [3]. *T.S.* 9, 1899, 193-5. Lists owners of the river banks in Leeds, Hunslet, Swillington, Castleforth, Ferry Bridge, Beale, Kellington, Haddlesey and Weeland.

Aiskew

See Bedale

Aldborough

LAWSON-TANCRED, THOS., SIR. *Records of a Yorkshire manor.* Edward Arnold & Co., 1936. Aldborough; includes many extracts from court rolls and other manorial records, *etc.*

LAWSON-TANCRED, THOMAS, SIR, & WALTER, J.W., eds. 'Extracts from the court rolls of the manor of Aldborough, 12-13 Edward III (1338-9)', in *Miscellanea* 2. Y.A.S., R.S., 74. 1929.

LAWSON TANCRED, T., SIR. 'Three seventeenth century court rolls of the manor of Aldborough', *Y.A.J.* 35, 1941-2, 201-16.

LAWSON-TANCRED, THOMAS, SIR. 'Extracts from the Aldborough court call', *Y.A.J.* 35, 1934, 321-5. List of suitors, late 18th c.

Allerton

'Charters relating to the possession of Kirkstall Abbey in Allerton', in *Miscellanea* [2]. *T.S.* 4, 1895, 42-59. Medieval.
See also Leeds

Askwith

PICKLES, MAY, & BOSWICK, JOSÉ. 'Farmhold structure in a district of piecemeal enclosure: the manor of Askwith from 1596 to 1816', *Y.A.J.* 63, 1991, 109-26. Includes list of tenants in 1596, and of 35 parties to an indenture of 1716.

Austwick

See Ingleton

Awborne

See Hunmanby

Baildon

BAILDON, WILLIAM PALEY. *Baildon and the Baildons: a history of a Yorkshire manor and family.* 3 vols. St. Catherine Press, 1912-27. Vol. 1 is devoted to the manor, and includes accounts of various different families. Vols. 2-3 are devoted to the Baildon family. Extensive.

Bainbridge

HALL, D.S. 'The manor of Bainbridge', *North Riding Record Office report* 1968, 39-47.

Barnsley

See Worsborough

Barton

BISHOP, T.A.M. 'An extent of Barton in Richmondshire', *Y.A.J.* 32, 1936, 86-97.

Barwick in Elmet

COOK, ROBERT B. 'Some old deeds relating to Barwick-in-Elmet', in *Miscellanea* [6]. *T.S.* 22, 1915, 174-82. Medieval-18th c.

LANCASTER, W.T., ed. 'Fifteenth century rentals of Barwick and Scholes', in *Miscellanea* [9]. *T.S.* 28, 1928, 238-54.

Battersby

See Stokesley

Bawtry

SHORT, CYNTHIA. 'Some notes on the Crewe muniments', *National Register of Archives: South Yorkshire Committee bulletin* 7, 1975, 3-5. Relating to Bawtry.

Beale

See Airedale

Bedale

'The Beresford-Piers archive', *North Riding Record Office report* 1966, 21-4. Description of estate archives relating to Bedale and Aiskew.

Bentley

See Wharfedale

Bilsdale

ASHCROFT, M.Y., & HILL, AUDREY M., eds. *Bilsdale surveys 1637-1851.* N.Y.C.R.O.P., 23, 1980. Estate surveys 1637, 1642, 1781, 1814 and 1826, with census 1851.

Birkby
See Hutton Bonville

Bishop Burton
ROGERS, MIKE. 'A new acquisition at the Humberside County Record Office', in CROWTHER, JAN, & CROWTHER, PETER, eds. *Collected articles from the Bulletin of the East Yorkshire Local History Society Bulletin, nos.1-55, 1970-Feb.1997.* [ ]: The Society, 1997, vol.2, 44-5. Originally published in the *Bulletin* **51**, 1994/5, 6-7. Discussion of manorial court rolls for South Burton (Bishop Burton), 1371-1642.

Bishop Monkton
'Landowners and occupiers 1841: Bishop Monkton', *Y.A.S., F.H.P.S.S.N.* **7**, 1974, 5. List of surnames.

Bolling
PRIEST, SYLVIA C. 'A Bolling household book, 1669-1687', *B.A.* **10**; N.S. **8**, 1962, 130-46.

Bradford
FEDERER, CHARLES A. 'West Riding cartulary: a collection of ancient documents, chiefly of the Hemingway mss', *B.A.* N.S. **1**, 1900, 26-44, 255-71, 384-95, & 541-50; **2**, 1905, 22-32, 190-204, 238-45 & 385-97; **3**, 1912, 26-36 & 122-32. 83 deed abstracts from the Bradford area.
LISTER, JOHN. 'Ancient charters from the Hemingway mss.', *B.A.* **1**, 1888, 210-7 & 274-9; **2**, 1895, 23-7, 106-10 & 209-15. Medieval deeds of the Bradford district.
ROBERTSHAW, WILFRED, ed. *West Yorkshire deeds.* Local record series 2. Bradford: Bradford Historical Society, 1936. 15-18th c., relating to Bradford and district.
EMPSALL, T.T. 'Bradford from the 14th to the 16th century, as seen through the account rolls of the manor', *B.A.* **2**, 1895, 72-80.
LISTER, JOHN. 'Chapter House records B2/19, P.R.O.', *B.A.* **2**, 1895, 57-65 & 137-47. Extent of the manor of Bradford, 1341.
SPEIGHT, H. 'The Bradford manor court rolls', *B.A.* N.S. **3**, 1912, 185-99. General discussion, with list of surviving rolls, 14-17th c.

CUDWORTH, WILLIAM. 'Old Bradford records: Bradford glebelands', *B.A.* **2**, 1895, 185-9. Includes sale particulars, 1794, listing tenants.

Brampton
JACKSON, CHARLES. 'Abstracts of old deeds', *Y.A.J.* **6**, 1881, 58-72. Medieval; mainly relating to Brampton.

Brandsburton
'Brandsburton', *B.T.* **12**, 1982, 6-8. Includes list of tenants, 1732, and tenants present at view of frankpledge, 1759, *etc.,* also list of estate papers at the Corporation of London Record Office.

Bretton Hall
PEARCE, CYRIL. 'The Bretton estate', *O.W.R.* 3(1), 1983, 24-8; 3(2), 1983, 10-23.
ADDY, JOHN, & GIBSON, ELIZABETH. 'Documentary: a fourteenth century rental from Bretton Hall', *O.W.R.* 5(1), 1985, 33-5.

Bridlington
INGRAM, M. EDWARD. *The manor of Bridlington and its lords feofees.* Bridlington: The Lords Feoffees, 1977.
PURVIS, J.S., ed. *Bridlington charters, court rolls and papers, XVIth – XIXth century, being a selection of documents illustrating the history of Bridlington under the lords feoffees.* A. Brown & Sons, 1926.

Brighouse
ARMYTAGE, GEORGE JOHN. 'Extracts from Mr. Roger Dodsworth's manuscripts relating to Brighouse, Clifton, Kirklees, and Hartshead, in the Wapentake of Morley, in the West Riding of the County of York', *Y.A.J.* **6**, 1881, 73-9. Medieval deeds, *etc.*
CLAY, H.T. 'Manor of Brighouse rentals, 1692-1736', *T. Hal. A.S.* 1943, 69-84.
CLAY, H.T. 'Manor of Brighouse court rolls, 1742-1793', *T. Hal A.S.* 1943, 45-68. 18th c.

Bromhead

HUNTER, JOSEPH. 'A memoir on the collection of charters and other documentary matter, illustrative of the topography and history of England, but especially of the County of York, made by John Wilson of Bromhead between 1753 and 1783', *Y.A.J.* **5**, 1879, 111-25. Includes 'a schedule of the deeds which relate to the estate of Bromhead, and to the Wilsons, its proprietors'.

Burton Agnes

COLLIER, C.V., ed. 'Burton Agnes', in *Miscellanea* **2**. Y.A.S., R.S., **74**. 1929, 87-99. Transcript of a 'book of paines and orders', 1632, with names of many inhabitants.

Bywater

See Leeds

Cadeby

CROSSLEY, E.W. 'The preceptory of Newland: the manor of Cadeby', *Y.A.J.* **35**, 1943, 139-56. Includes rentals, 1662 and 1755, various letters, *etc.*, 17-18th c.

Calverley

BAILDON, WILLIAM PALEY, & MARGERISON, SAMUEL, eds. *The Calverley charters presented to the British Museum by Sir Walter Calverley Trevelyan, Baronet, volume 1.* T.S. **6**. 1904. No more published. The charters primarily relate to medieval Calverley, Pudsey, and Farsley, owned by the Calverley family.

'Survey of the manor of Calverley & Farsley, and also several estates in Bramley and Pudsey, July 1810', *Y.F.H.* **14**(2), 1988, 35-6. Surnames of the tenants of Thomas Thornhill.

Castleforth

See Airedale

Clapham

See Ingleton

Cleveland

HARRISON, B.J.D. 'Some documentary sources for the history of housing', *C.T.L.H.S.B.* **16**, 1972, 1-5. In the Cleveland area.

Clifforth

See Thwate

Clifton

CRUMP, W.B. 'Clifton and its common field: a survey in 1788', *P.R.H.A.S.* 1925, 105-35 Includes names of tenants.

See also Brighouse

Cowthorp

JACKSON, CHARLES. 'Local muniments: abstracts of deeds in the possession of James Montagu, esq., of Melton-on-the-Hill, near Doncaster', *Y.A.J.* **5**, 1879, 227-40. Medieval deeds of Cowthorp.

Conisborough

HOYLE, WILLIAM FRETWELL. 'Abstract of the title to the manor of Coningsborough in the County of York', *Y.A.J.* **9**, 1886, 216-20. 16-18th c.

Cookridge

See Adel

Cottingham

KNIGHT, WINIFRED I. 'Housing development in the c.19-20 in the area of Cottingham bounded on the south by South Street, on the east by King Street, on the north by Finkle Street and on the West by Baynard Avenue', *Cottingham Local History Society journal* **16**(1), 1995, 5-56. Includes names of many owners and tenants, with extracts from electoral registers.

Coverham

POLLARD, A.J., & ASHCROFT, M.Y. 'Coverham: some fifteenth century manorial records', *Journal* **10**; N.Y.C.R.O.P. **35**, 1984, 29-43.

Cowley

See Ecclesfield

Dallowgill Moor

See Grewelthorpe Moor

Danby

NATTRASS, MARY. 'Some freehold farms and the manor of Danby', *C.T.L.H.S.B.* **27**, 1974-5, 19-26. Notes on a sale of farms in 1655.

Delph

WRIGHT, DANNIE. 'The sale of the Delph estate of Ralph Lawton in 1856', *B.S.H.S.* **23**(4), 1993, 23-7. Sale particulars include names of tenants of 32 lots.

Dewsbury

CHADWICK, S.J. 'The Dewsbury Moot Hall', *Y.A.J.* **21**, 1910-11, 345-478. See also **22**, 1913, 126. Includes transcript of the Dewsbury Rectory account rolls, 1348-56, and court rolls, late 16th c.

BROADBENT, JOHN F. 'Dewsbury inclosure, 1796-1806', *Y.A.J.* **69**, 1997, 209-26. Includes brief list of the 'principal freeholders'

Dinnington

See Tankersley

Doncaster

THEOBALD, CHAS. H. 'Extracts from a Doncaster court roll of the sixteenth century', *Y.A.J.* **35**, 1943, 288-310.

Easby

See Stokesley

East Witton

See Hunmanby

Ecclesall

WIGFULL, JAMES R. 'Her Majesties manor of Ecclesall', *T. Hunter A.S.* **4**, 1937, 28-45. Depositions made in 1587.

Ecclesfield

'William West, the seneschal of Hallamshire', in HALL, T. WALTER. *South Yorkshire historical sketches.* Sheffield: J.W. Northend, 1931, 16-61. Extracts from court rolls of Ecclesfield, Cowley and Sheffield, 15-16th c.

Eckington

GARRATT, H.J.H., ed. *Eckington: the court rolls, V: 1694-1804.* Huddersfield: the editor, 1997. Vols I-IV not yet published in 1999. Extensive calendar.

See also Worsborough

Edlington

See Hunmanby

Elmswell

WOODWARD, DONALD., ed. *The farming and memorandum books of Henry Best of Elmswell, 1642.* Records of social and economic history, N.S., **8**. O.U.P., 1984, Includes a few Elmswell probate records and manorial documents, with a pedigree of Best, 17th c.

Elslack

T., J.F. 'Charters relating to Elslack and Glusbourne, in Craven, Co. York, with a pedigree of their descent in the families of Darell, Marton, De Alta Ripa (or Dautry), Radcliffe, and Malhome, and pedigrees of Vavasur, Reuell, Sutton, Wratham, Clusburne, etc', *Collectanea topographica et genealogica* **6**, 1840, 123-47 & 301-33. 196 deeds, 13-17th c.

Eston

See Greenhow

Etton

HALL, T. WALTER. *Etton: an East Yorkshire village.* Sheffield: J.W. Northend, 1932. Calendar of 81 charters, with genealogical notes.

Exley

BRIGG, WM. ANDERTON. 'The forgotten manor of Exley', *B.A.* N.S. **3**, 1912, 97-114. Includes extracts from court rolls, *etc.,* medieval-18th c.

See also Harden

Fanshawe Gate

See Tankersley

Farnley

HORWOOD, ALFRED J. 'The manuscripts of Ayscough Fawkes, esq., of Farnley Hall, Co.York', in *Seventh report of the Royal Commission on Historical Manuscripts, Part 1. Report and appendix.* H.M.S.O., 1879, 509-11. Estate records, medieval, including deeds relating to Fountains Abbey.

Farsley

See Calverley

Ferry Bridge
See Airedale

Fingall
See Hunmanby

Firbeck
See Tickhill

Garforth
'Allotments and awards under the Garforth Enclosure Act', in *Thoresby Miscellany* 11. *T.S.* 37, 1945, 105-31. 1810; lists landowners.

Garton
TOWSE, CLIVE. *An account of an estate in Garton and the East Riding of Yorkshire, the property of the Towse family 1537-1800, with a note on the Somerset branch of the family.* Cardiff: the author, 1980. Includes pedigree.

Gusburn
See Elslack

Gomersal
'Local muniments', *Y.A.J.* 3, 1875, 64-80. Abstracts of 16-17th c. deeds relating to Gomersal, Leeds, *etc.*, and to the families of Pygott, Norcliffe, Pawson, Brooke and Atkinson, *etc.*

Grantley
HEBDEN, JOHN. 'Grantley estates survey of 1827', *R.H.* 2 (5), 1994, 114-7. Lists tenants.

Greenhow
HARRISON, B.J.D. 'Some Cleveland court rolls of Lord Darcy and Meynell, 1406-11', *C.T.L.H.S.B.* 1, 1968, unpaginated, 2, 1968, 7-8. Extracts from court rolls of Greenhow, Eston, Hutton Rudby, and Seamer.

Grewelthorpe Moor
HEBDEN, JOHN. 'The enclosure of Grewelthorpe Moor and the inhabitants of Kirkby Malzeard: a Star Chamber lawsuit, 1598', *R.H.* 1(5), 1991, 11-14. Includes list of names.

HEBDEN, JOHN. 'The Grewelthorpe and Dallowgill Moor enclosure riots of the early 1600s', *R.H.* 1(4), 1990, 5-7. Includes list of persons accused of 'riot', 1607-8.

Gringley
See Tickhill

Hackness
WALKER, J.W., ed. *Hackness manuscripts and accounts.* Y.A.S., R.S., **95**. 1938. Accounts of John Van den Bempde, 1658-1728, extracts from Lady Margaret Hoby's diary, 1599-1605, Hoby wills, 16-17th c., etc. Includes pedigree showing relationship of Hoby and Sydenham, 16-17th c., also of Van den Bempde, 15-20th c.

Haddlesey
See Airedale

Halifax
ROBERTSHAW, WILFRED. 'The Horton collection of manuscripts', *T. Hal. A.S.* 1956, 59-60. Description of an estate archive of the Halifax area.

MORGAN, LESLIE. 'Halifax deeds and documents in the Lancashire County Record Office, 1335-1806', *T. Hal. A.S.* 1971, 29-31. Brief description of two collections of Halifax deeds.

ELLIS, MARTHA J. 'A study in the manorial history of Halifax parish in the sixteenth and early seventeenth centuries', *Y.A.J.* **40**, 1962, 250-64 & 420-42.

KENDALL, H.P. 'The rental of the freeholders and copyholders of Halifax, 1587-8', *T. Hal. A.S.* 1930, 9-45.

Hallamshire
HALL, T.W., ed. *Descriptive catalogue of early charters relating to lands in and near Sheffield, with illustrations, genealogies & notes.* Sheffield: J.W. Northend, 1938.

HALL, T. WALTER. *Sheffield and its environs, 13th to the 17th century: a descriptive catalogue of land charters & other documents forming the Brooke Taylor collection relating to the outlying districts of Sheffield, with 16 genealogies and an article on Hawskyard.* Sheffield: J.W. Northend, 1922.

HALL, THOMAS WALTER. *Sheffield and Rotherham from the 12th to the 18th century: a descriptive catalogue of miscellaneous charters and other documents relating to the districts of Sheffield and Rotherham, with abstracts of Sheffield wills proved at York from 1544 to 1560, and 315 genealogies deduced therefrom.* Sheffield: J.W. Northend, 1916.

HALL, THOMAS WALTER. *A descriptive catalogue of ancient charters & instruments relating to lands near Sheffield in the counties of York, Derby, Nottingham and Lincoln, with genealogies and notes.* Sheffield: Northend, 1935.

WALTON, MARY. 'List of manorial records relating to the neighbourhood of Sheffield, in repositories or libraries other than the Sheffield City Libraries', *T. Hunter A.S.* **5**, 1943, 96-8. Includes listing of Derbyshire records, as well as South Yorkshire.

Handsworth Woodhouse

ADDY, S.O. 'Documents relating to Handsworth Woodhouse', *Y.A.J.* **20**, 1908-9, 6-19. Deeds abstracts, 14-17th c.

Harden

WHONE, CLIFFORD. 'The Paslew estate in Harden and Exley', *B.A.* **10**; N.S. **8**, 1962, 39-67. Includes survey, 1570, and abstracts of deeds.

Harrop Edge

'The enclosure of Harrop Edge', *B.S.H.S.* **14**(1), 1984, 10-12. Includes list of purchasers, undated.

Hartshead

See Brighouse

Hatfield Chase

COLLIER, C.V., ed. 'Stovin's manuscript', *T.E.R.A.S.* **12**, 1905, 23-60; **13**(2), 1906, 197-245. An account of the drainage of Hatfield Chase, 18th c.; includes names of many landowners etc.

JACKSON, CHARLES. 'The Stovin manuscript', *Y.A.J.* **7**, 1882, 194-238. History of the drainage of the levels of Hatfield Chase; includes part of the Huguenot register of Sandtoft, Lincolnshire, 1643-85.

Hawksyard

See Hallamshire

Haworth

WHONE, CLIFFORD, ed. *Court rolls of the manor of Haworth.* Local record series **3**. Bradford: Bradford Historical & Antiquarian Society, 1946. Transcripts, 1581-1870.

Healaugh

ALLISON, K.J. 'Enclosure by agreement at Healaugh (W.R.)', *Y.A.J.* **40**, 1962, 382-91. Includes list of tenants, 1636.

Helmsley

'The Feversham (Duncombe) family archives', *Journal* **1**; N.Y.C.R.O.P. **1**, 1975, 19-28. Lists estate archives of the Duncombe family, Earls of Feversham, mainly relating to Helmsley and Kirbymoorside, 18th c.

Hessay

NEWMAN, P.R. 'The Hessay enclosure of 1831: a study in the economic and social history of an Ainsty township in the 19th century', *Journal* **9**; N.Y.C.R.O.P. **29**, 1982, 89-165. Includes census returns, 1841-71.

High Sunderland

'High Sunderland', *Y.N.Q.I.* **1**, 1888, 68-73. Deed abstracts, 18-19th c.

Hipperholme

See Rastrick

Holbeck

LUMB, G.D. 'Anderton rents, 1708', in *Miscellanea* **[8]**. *T.S.* **26**, 1924, 163-4. Rents charged on lands in Holbeck. *See also* Leeds

Horsforth

LANCASTER, W.T. 'The early history of Horsforth', in *Miscellanea* [5]. *T.S.* **15**, 1909, 222-50. Includes 9 medieval charters, and a survey of the Horsforth estates of Kirkstall Abbey, c.1539-41.

Hull

HORROX, ROSMARY, ed. *Selected rentals and accounts of medieval Hull, 1293-1528.* Y.A.S., R.S. **141**. 1983.

SHEPPARD, T. 'Historical documents relating to Hull & district', *T.E.R.A.S.* **28**, 1939, 153-67. Lists 259 deeds, etc., in a Hull museum.

BILSON, JOHN. 'Wyke-upon-Hull in 1293', *T.E.R.A.S.* **26**, 1929, 37-105. Includes names from 1293 rental; this is the old name for Hull.

HORROX, ROSEMARY. *The changing plan of Hull, 1290-1650: a guide to documentary sources for the early topography of Hull.* Hull: Kingston upon Hull City Council, 1978. Maps property boundaries, naming owners, tenants, *etc.*

WOODWARD, DONALD. 'The accounts of the building of Trinity House, Hull', *Y.A.J.* **62**, 1990, 153-70.

ALLISON, K.J. *"Hull gent seeks country residence', 1750-1850.* E.Y.L.H.S. **36**. 1981. Gazetteer of country houses in the Hull region, with lists of owners and occupiers.

Hunmanby

BOULTER, W.C. 'Court-rolls of some East Riding manors, 1563-1573', *Y.A.J.* **10**, 1889, 63-82 & 407-22. Relating to Hunmanby, Awborne, Settrington, and Nafferton, Temple Hirst, Temple Newsham, Fingall, Edlington, East Witton and West Scrafton.

Hunslet

See Airdale

Hutton Bonville

'Manor of Hutton Bonville in Birkby parish, Allertonshire, North Riding of Yorkshire', *Topographer & genealogist* **1**, 1846, 509-12.

Hutton Rudby

See Greenhow

Idle

YEWDALL, MR. 'Free rents of Idle for one year', *Y.A.S., F.H.P.S.S.N.* **7**(2), 1981, 117-8. Undated rental.

'Manor or lordship of Idle, A.D. 1584', *B.A.* **1**, 1888, 192-200 & 267-73. Survey.

Ingleby

See Stokesley

Ingleton

HOYLE, R.W. 'Lords, tenants, and tenant right in the sixteenth century', *N.H.* **20**, 1984, 38-63. Study of Ingleton, Newby, Clapham and Austwick.

Keighley

JUDSON, H.I. 'Keighley chantry lands', *B.A.* **9**; N.S., **7**, 1952, 55-60. Includes list of tenants, 1568.

SMITH, T.K. 'The Duke's steward: some problems in Keighley manor in the eighteenth century', *O.W.R.* **5**(2), 1985, 7-11.

Kellington

See Airedale

Kippax

See Leeds

Kirby in Cleveland

See Stokesley

Kirkby Malzeard

See Grewelthorpe Morr

Kirkby Moorside

See Helmsley

Kirkby under Knoll

D., R. 'Early charters relating to the manor of Kirkby-under-Knoll, in the North Riding of Yorkshire', *Topographer & genealogist* **1**, 1846, 216-23.

Kirklees

'Kirklees charters', *Y.A.J.* **16**, 1900-1901, 464-6. Medieval.

See also Brighouse

Knaresborough

THOMAS, SYLVIA. 'A Knaresborough account, 1421-1422', *O.W.R.* 3(1), 1983, 30-2.

Laughton

See Tickhill

Ledston

See Leeds

Leeds

LE PATOUREL, JOHN, ed. *Documents relating to the manor and borough of Leeds, 1066-1400.* T.S. **45**. 1956.

KIRBY, JOAN W., ed. *The manor and borough of Leeds, 1425-1662: an edition of documents.* T.S. **57**. 1981.

LISTER, JOHN, ed. 'Chapter House records', in *Miscellanea* [10]. *T.S.* **33**, 1935, 83-102. Extents, 1341, of Leeds, Rothwell, Allerton, Bywater, Kippax and Ledston; translated from Latin.

LANCASTER, W.T. 'A fifteenth century rental of Leeds', in *Miscellanea* [7]. *T.S.* **24**, 1919, 6-22.

MARSHALL, THOMAS. 'Chartae Leodinenses, with notes on the Reame family and the Leeds chantries of the B.V.M.', in *Miscellanea* [2]. *T.S.* **4**, 1895, 65-78. Transcript of deed relating to the Saddle Inn, Leeds, 1602, with details of descent.

KELSEY, H.T. 'Survey of the manor of Leeds', in *Miscellanea* [4]. *T.S.* **11**, 1904, 369-437. See also *Miscellanea* 7. *T.S.* **24**, 1919, 336-44. Taken in 1612.

'Leeds in 1628: a 'ridinge observation' from the City of London', in BERESFORD, M.W. *Time and place: collected essays.* Hambledon Press, 1985, 293-307. Discussion and transcript of a 1628 survey of the manor of Leeds. Originally published in *N.H.* **10**, 1975, 126-40.

LUMB, G.D. 'Abstract of the Leeds manor rolls, 1650-1666, probably made for the steward's use, and annotated by him', in *Miscellanea* [3]. *T.S.* **9**, 1899, 63-80.

LANCASTER, W.T. 'The manor court of Leeds Kirkgate-cum-Holbeck', in *Miscellanea* [8]. *T.S.* **26**, 1924, 129-47. Proceedings, 1666-72.

LUMB, G.D. 'Observations out of the mannour booke of Leeds, which begins the 5th of May, '84', in *Miscellanea* [3]. *T.S.* **9**, 1899, 278-98.

See also Airedale and Gomersal

Lindley

DAVEY, PETER. 'Manor of Lindley: perambulation of the bounds', *Wh. N.* **26**, 1997, 14-15. Includes list of boys of Lindley and Stainburn who perambulated the bounds of the manor in 1762.

Little Kelk

HALE, ROBERT. 'Account roll of the manor of Little Kelk, 1323-4. *Y.A.J.* **63**, 1991, 59-76.

Longshaw

See Tankersley

Malton

SALMON, D.J., ed. *Malton in the early nineteenth century.* N.Y.C.R.O.P. **26**, 1981. Includes an estate survey, 1840s.

Manningham

ROBERTSHAW, WILFRED. 'The township of Manningham in the nineteenth century', *B.A.* **8**; N.S. **6**, 1940, 57-89. Includes survey, 1613.

Middleham

See Wensleydale

Middlesbrough

'Extract from deed of covenants dated February 8th 1831: schedule of persons purchasing land', *C.T.L.H.S.B.* **1**, 1968, unpaginated. Presumably in Middlesbrough.

Monk Friston

BISHOP, T.A.M., ed. 'Extent of Monk Friston, 1320', in *Miscellanea* 4. Y.A.S., R.S. **94**, 1937, 39-72 & 175-89.

Morton

'A valuation of the manor of Morton, and as occupied in 1792', *K.D.F.H.S.J.* Spring 1997, 18-19. Lists owners and occupiers.

Murgatroyd

R., C.A. 'Murgatroyd evidences', *Northern genealogist* **6**, 1903, 39-41. Deeds, 16-17th c.

Myton

TRAVIS-COOK, J. *Notes relative to the manor of Myton.* Hull: A. Brown & Sons, 1890. Medieval.

Nafferton

See Hunmanby

Newby

See Ingleton

Newsome

See Thwate

Nidderdale

See Wharfedale

Northallerton

FOWLER, J.T. 'On certain *Starrs,* or Jewish documents, partly relating to Northallerton', *Y.A.J.* **3**, 1875, 55-63. Medieval deeds.

Oglethorpe

See Thwate

Osmotherley Moor

ATKINSON, D.A. 'Osmotherley Moor enclosure act', *J.Cl.F.H.S.* **4**(4), 1989, 28-32. Lists commissioners, landowners, and tenants of cottages, 1755.

Otley

KIRK, G.E. 'Two rentals of the manor of Otley', in *Thoresby miscellany* **[11]**. *T.S.* **37**, 1945, 202-24. 1692 and 1695.

Owlerton

'Owlerton manor', in HALL, T. WALTER. *South Yorkshire historical sketches.* Sheffield: J.W. Northend, 1931, 85-116. Extracts from manorial records, 14-18th c. *See also* Sheffield

Patrington

MADDOCK, H.E. 'Court rolls of Patrington manors', *T.E.R.A.S.* **8**, 1900, 10-35.

ALEXANDER, ANN, CASPERSON, FRED, HABBERSON, MOIRA, HALL, MARY, & PICKLES, MAY. 'Patrington: a fifteenth-century manorial account', *Y.A.J.* **62**, 1990, 141-52.

Pickering

TURTON, ROBERT BELL, ed. *The honor and forest of Pickering.* 4 vols. North Riding Record Society N.S., **1-4**. 1894-7. Includes surveys, inquisitions, deeds, subsidies, accounts, petitions, *etc., etc.*

CROSSLEY, E.W. 'The rectory of Pickering: a chapter in its history', *Y.A.J.* **35**, 1943, 404-23. Not completed. Includes a list of tenants, 1643, rentals, 1678 and 1679 *etc.*

Pocklington

BELLINGHAM, ROGER A. 'Mr Powell's enclosure award and the computer', *Local historian* **25**(2), 1995, 77-87. Computer analysis of the 1759 enclosure award for Pocklington.

Pontefract

LUMB, G.D. 'A fifteenth century rental of Pontefract', *Miscellanea* **[8]**. *T.S.* **22**, 1915, 253-73.

Pudsey

See Calverley

Rastrick

CLAY, H. TRAVIS. 'Early inhabitants of Rastrick', *T. Hal. A.S.* 1948, 27-37; 1952, 59-64. Includes medieval deed abstracts.

LISTER, J., ed. *The extent (or survey) of the graveships of Rastrick, Hipperholme and Sowerby, 1309.* Halifax Antiquarian Society record series **2**. 1914.

'Rastrick grave rental, 1710-1836', *T. Hal. A.S.* 1929, 285-303.

Reighton

COLLIER, C.V. 'Reighton manor', in *Miscellanea* 2. Y.A.S., R.S. **74**. 1929, 100-103. Transcript of 'pains laid and orders agreed', 1726, with list of signatories.

Ribston

'Ribston and the Knights Templars', *Y.A.J.* **7**, 1882, 429-52; **8**, 1884, 259-99; **9**, 1886, 71-98. Medieval deeds.

Richmond

WENHAM, L.P., ed. *Richmond burgage houses, North Yorkshire: surveys of 1679, 1773 & 1820.* N.Y.C.R.O.P. **16**. 1978.

Richmondshire

GALE, ROGER, ed. *Registrum Honoris de Richmond, exhibens terrarum & villarum quæ quandum fuerunt Edwini Comitus infra Richmundshire descriptionem, ex libro Domesday in thesauria Domini Regis, necnon varias extentas, feoda comitis, feoda militum, relevia, fines & wardas, inquisitiones, compotos, clamea, chartasque ad Richmondiæ comitatum spectantes. Omnia juxta exemplar antiquum in Bibliotheca Cottoniana asservatum exarata. Adjiciuntur in appendice chartæ aliæ, observationes plurimæ, genealogicæ, & indices ad opus illustrandum necessarii.* R.Gosling, 1722.
See also Wensleydale

Rievaulx Abbey

COPPACK, GLYN. 'Some descriptions of Rievaulx Abbey in 1538-9: the disposition of a major Cistercian precinct in the early sixteenth century', *Journal of the British Archaeological Association* **139**, 1986, 100-33. Includes surveys, naming tenants.

Ripon

'Some properties of the Duchy of Lancaster in Ripon, 1549-1576', *R.H.* **2**(6), 1994, 141-4. Lists tenants.
'A group of leaseholders and sub-tenants in Ripon, c. 1618/1619', *R.H.* **1**(1), 1988, 8-11. Survey of estate of Ripon's Free Grammar School; many names of tenants.

Roecliffe

LAWSON-TANCRED, THOMAS, SIR. 'Records of Roecliffe', *Y.A.J.* **34**, 1939, 317-28. Includes descent, accounts, 1406 and 1547, extracts from court rolls, 1354-1601, lists of tenants in 1300 and 1803, poll tax 1379, *etc.*

Rotherham

'Extracts from grants of Rotherham manor', *T. Hunter A.S.* **2**(1), 1920, 30-38. Medieval-17th c.

PRESTON, W.M.E. 'Two seventeenth-century Yorkshire rentals', *Y.A.J.* **34**, 1929, 329-41. For Rotherham, 1654 and 1649.
See also Hallamshire

Rothwell

LANCASTER, W.T.L. 'A fifteenth century rental of Rothwell', in *Miscellanea* **[7]**. *T.S.* **24**, 1919, 281-303.
HOYLE, R.W. 'Thomas Lord Darcy and the Rothwell tenants, 1526-1534', *Y.A.J.* **63**, 1991, 85-107. Early 16th c.
See also Leeds

Roundhay

MORKILL, JOHN W. 'The manor and park of Roundhay', in *Miscellanea* **1**. *T.S.* **2**, 1891, 215-48. Includes folded pedigree of Sagar-Musgrave of Bramley and Red Hall, 17-19th c.

Saddleworth

'Old Saddleworth', *B.S.H.S. passim.* Most issues of this *bulletin* includes information on the descent of particular properties in Saddleworth.
'Saddleworth records part 2: deeds and papers relating to Saddleworth in the Cornwall-Legh manuscripts in the John Rylands Library, Manchester', *B.S.H.S.* **10**(3), 1980, 50-53. Deed abstracts, 16-17th c.
BARNES, B., et al, eds. *Saddleworth surveyed: selected maps of the township, 1625-1851.* Saddleworth: Saddleworth Historical Society, 1983. Includes various lists of names from estate and enclosure maps.
BARNES, B. 'Manor records', *B.S.H.S.* **5-8**, 1975-8. *passim.* 18th c.
PETFORD, ALAN. 'Some Saddleworth court rolls', *B.S.H.S.* **14-16**, 1984-5, *passim.* Includes extracts, 18th c.
'Saddleworth court rolls', *B.S.H.S.* **19**(4), 1989, 12-15. Transcript for 1757.
'Manor records: Saddleworth enclosure', *B.S.H.S.* **8**, 1978, 27-9, 43-52, 61-8, 112-15; **9**(1), 1979, 33-9. Early 19th c., many names of tenants *etc.*
PETFORD, A.J. 'Saddleworth records, part 3. Documents relating to the Saddleworth Enclosure Act of 1810', *B.S.H.S.* **10**(14), 1980, 68-77.

Scarborough

L., L.B. 'Grant of Matilda, widow of Adam Brus of Pickering, of land in Scarborough to the Friars Minor of that town, 1323', *Collectanea topographica et genealogica* **4**, 1837, 312.

Scholes

See Barwick in Elmet

Seamer

See Greenhow

Sedburgh

PATTENDEN, D.W. 'The manor and wapentake of Sadberge', *Cleveland history* **63**, 1992, 2-11. Includes lists of tenants in 1381 and 1778.

Settrington

KING, H., & HARRIS, A., eds. *A survey of the manor of Settrington.* Y.A.S., R.S., **126.** 1962. Made in 1600.
See also Hunmanby

Sheffield

HALL, THOMAS W. *Sheffield 1297 to 1554: catalogue of the ancient charters belonging to the twelve capital burgesses & commonalty of the town and parish of Sheffield, usually known as the church burgesses, with abstracts of all Sheffield wills proved at York prior to 1554.* Sheffield: J.W. Northend, 1913.

HALL, T. WALTER. *Sheffield, Hallamshire: a descriptive catalogue of Sheffield manorial records from the 8th year of Richard II to the Restoration.* Sheffield: J.W. Northend, 1926.

HALL, T. WALTER, ed. *A descriptive catalogue (2nd volume) of Sheffield manorial records and South-Yorkshire land charters from the Lindsay collection, and notes on Thundercliffe & the Hermitage of St John, with a list of mills on the Don & its tributaries.* Sheffield: J.W. Northend, 1928.

HALL, THOMAS WALTER, ed. *Sheffield, Hallamshire: a descriptive catalogue (3rd volume) of Sheffield manorial records from the court-roll, 1424 to 1497; also diverse ancient charters & instruments as*

to Sheffield, with notes on Owlerton Hall and index to liber finium. Sheffield: J.W. Northend, 1934.

'Records of the Court Baron of the manor of Sheffield', *T. Hunter A.S.* **1**(3-4), 1918, 257-329. Extracts, medieval-16th c.

POTTER, G.R., & WALTON, MARY. 'A fragment of a *compotus* roll of the manor of Sheffield, 1479-1480', *T. Hunter A.S.* **6**, 1950, 1-24.

THOMAS, A. H. 'Some Hallamshire rolls of the fifteenth century', *T. Hunter A.S.* **2**(1), 1920, 65-79; **2**(2), 1921, 142-8; **2**(3), 1922, 225-46; **2**(4), 1924, 341-60. Discussion of Sheffield manorial records, with transcripts of medieval accounts, *etc.*

'The court leet of the manor of Sheffield', *T. Hunter A. S.* **3**, 1929, 143-54. Includes amercements made in 1578, *etc.*

POSTLES, DAVID. *Sheffield in 1581.* Sheffield: Sheffield City Libraries, 1981. Transcript of the Earl of Shrewsbury's Hallamshire rental, 1581.

RONKSLEY, JAMES GEORGE, ed. *An exact and perfect view of the manor of Sheffield, with other lands, by John Harrison, 1637.* Worksop: Robert White & Co., 1908.

'Customs of the manor of Sheffield', *T. Hunter A.S.* **2**(4), 1924, 371-3. Includes list of jurors, 1650.

'The court leet of the manor of Sheffield', *T. Hunter A.S.* **1**(2), 1917, 193-203. Includes list of constables and other officers, 1795.

WILLIS, JOHN. 'Memorial of indentures dates 10th, 11th, 18th July 1815, of land and property in Angel Steet, Sheffield', *F.S.* **11**(4), 1991, 101-2.
See also Ecclesfield, Hallamshire and Worsborough

Shelf. Carr House Farm

METCALFE, CYRIL. 'The documents of Carr House Farm, Shelf, 1600-1794', *T. Hal. A.S.* N.S., **3**, 1995, 47-55. Discussion of its deeds.

Sherburn

ALEXANDRA, GEORGE GLOVER. 'The manorial system and copyhold tenure', in *Miscellanea* **[10]**. *T.S.* **33**, 1935, 283-305. Based on the records of the manor of Sherburn, 1739-61; includes will of Edward Squire, 1760.

Shibden Hall

COLLEDGE, ERIC. 'The medieval muniments of Shibden Hall', *T. Hal. A.S.* 1940, 67-82. General discussion.

GREEN, MURIEL M. 'The Shibden Hall muniments', *T. Hal. A.S.* 1938, 61-70.

LIDDINGTON, JILL. 'Gender, authority and mining in an industrial landscape: Anne Lister, 1791-1840', *History workshop journal* 42, 1996, 59-86. Discussion of Lister's estate management at Shibden.

Shipley

'A particular note of all the oxgangs in the towne of Shipley', *B.A.* 8; N.S., 6, 1940, 56. Lists occupiers.

'Shipley homage, circa 1644', *B.A.* 7; N.S., 5, 1933, 239. List of tenants.

Skyrack Wapentake

MORKILL, J.W. 'Notes on the Wapentake of Skyrack', in *Miscellanea* 1. *T.S.* 2, 1892, 115-41. Extracts from medieval deeds, *etc.*

Sledmere

ENGLISH, BARBARA. 'On the eve of the Great Depression: the economy of the Sledmere estate, 1869-1878', *Business history* 24(1), 24-47. Owned by the Sykes family, based on estate papers.

Snape

ASHCROFT, M.Y. 'Snape in the late fifteenth century: account rolls reproduced and translated', *Journal* 5; N.Y.C.R.O.P. 13, 1977, 20-58.

Sowerby

GREENWELL, W. 'Some Lascells deeds and evidences', *Y.A.J.* 2, 1873, 87-96. Deeds of the Lascells family of Sowerby, medieval.

KENDALL, H.P. 'Greave list of Sowerby for 1624', *T. Hal. A.S.* 1932, 29-68. Rental, with notes on many of the tenants listed. *See also* Rastrick

Soyland

PRIESTLEY, J.H. 'Two Soyland disputes', *T. Hal. A.S.* 1949, 61-70. Includes list of owners and occupiers of Sowerby and Soyland, 1760, engaged in dispute with the lord of the manor.

Stainburn

See Lindley

Stainsborough

See Worsborough

Stainton

ASHCROFT, M.Y. 'The records of a manor: the population of Stainton (by Downholme) in the middle of the 17th century', *C.T.L.H.S.B.* 16, 1972, 15-21; 18, 1972, 7-10. Traces tenants in the court rolls.

Staley

H., J.M. 'The Staley rental', *B.S.H.S.* 16(2), 1986, 38-42. Lists of tenants, 1397/8 and 1407-8.

Staxton

LOUGHBOROUGH, BRIAN. 'An account of a Yorkshire enclosure: Staxton, 1803', *Agricultural history review* 13, 1965, 106-15. Includes brief list of landowners.

Stokesley

HILL, AUDREY. 'Elizabethan court rolls for Stokesley, Kirby in Cleveland, Ingleby cum Battersby, & Easby', *C.T.L.H.S.B.* 12, 1971, 1-6. For 1577 and 1582.

Swaledale

ASLIN, M.S. 'An old Swaledale account book', *Dalesman* 10, 1948-9, 269-9. Discussion of the account book of Thomas Smale, 1730-39, subsquently used by H. Cheytor, 1845-6; includes list of wages paid 1845.

Swillington

See Airedale

Tankersley

HALL, T. WALTER. *A descriptive catalogue of charters and manorial records relating to lands in Tankersley, Fanshawe Gate, Dinnington & Longshaw, in the neighbourhood of Sheffield, with illustrations, genealogies & notes.* Sheffield: J.W. Northend, 1937.

Temple Hirst

See Hunmanby

Temple Newsam

KIRK, G.E., ed. 'A sixteenth century rental of the manor of Temple Newsam and its appurtenances', in *Miscellanea* [10]. *T.S.* 33, 1935, 61-70. 1507.

Temple Newsham

See Hunmanby

Thorner

LANCASTER, W.T. 'Fourteenth century court rolls of the manor of Thorner', in *Miscellanea* [5]. *T.S.* 15, 1909, 153-73.

Thorpe in Balne

BRISCOE, GILL. 'Thorpe-in-Balne manorial records in Doncaster Archive Department', *Don. Anc.* 1(3), 1981, 105-8. Includes names from the suit roll, 1784-1807.

Thundercliffe

See Sheffield

Thwate

T[URNER], J.H., & G., J.J. 'Fairfax mss', *Y.C.M.* 2, 1892, 234-9. Extracts from manorial court rolls of Thwate cum Newsome, 1567, and Towton with Clifforth cum Oglethorpe, late 16th c.

Tickhill

'The castle & honour of Tickhill, Co. York, the Duchy of Lancaster: court-roll of Tickhill, Firbeck, Gringley & Laughton, 1597 to 1601', in HALL, T. WALTER. *South Yorkshire historical sketches.* Sheffield: J.W. Northend, 1931, 62-84.

Tinsley

BATLEY, LILIAN. 'The rolls of the great court baron of Tinsley', *T. Hunter A.S.* 9(2), 1966, 61-74. General discussion, with notes on the families of Swyft, Shepley, Stainforth, and Bright.

POSTLES, DAVID. 'Tinsley rentals, 1336-1514', *Y.A.J.* 51, 1979, 51-60.

Towton

See also Thwate

Underbank

'Horsfall deeds: Underbank, near Hebden Bridge', *Y.C.M.* 1, 1891, 324-7. 16-19th c.

Wakefield

Wakefield was one of the largest manors in England; its lands included not just the township of Wakefield itself, but also places as far distant as Holme, Heptonstall and Eccleshill, and covered a considerable proportion of the West Riding, occupying most of the Wapentakes of Agbrigg and Morley. A general study of the manor is provided by:

O'REGAN, MARY. *The medieval manor court of Wakefield.* Leeds: Rosalba Press, 1994.

See also:

TAYLOR, THOMAS. *The history of Wakefield in the County of York: the Rectory Manor, with biographical and other notices of some of the persons connected therewith.* Wakefield: W.H. Milnes, 1886. Includes extensive extracts from manorial records. The Rectory Manor was separated from the manor of Wakefield in the eleventh century.

The extensive records of the manor are described in:

MICHELMORE, DAVID J.H., & EDWARDS, MARGARET K.E. 'The records of the manor of Wakefield', *Journal of the Society of Archivists.* 5(4), 1975, 245-50.

Other general works include:

'Genealogical notes from Wakefield manor rolls', *Y.N.Q.I.* 2, 1890, 294-304. Extracts, 1272-1306.

'Greves, graves or prepositi', *Y.G.* 1, 1888, 34-9, 64-6 & 203-8. List of graves, i.e. bailiffs of Wakefield manor, 13-16th c.

JEWELL, HELEN M. 'Women at the courts of the manor of Wakefield, 1348-1350', *N.H.* 26, 1990, 59-81.

Quite a number of manorial court rolls, *etc.,* have been published; they are listed here chronologically.

1274-97

BAILDON, WILLIAM PALEY. ed. *Court rolls of the manor of Wakefield, vol. 1. 1274-1297.* Y.A.S., R.S. 29. 1901.

1286
See 1313-16

1297-1309
BAILDON, WILLIAM PALEY, ed. *Court rolls of the manor of Wakefield, vol. II. 1297 to 1309.* Y.A.S., R.S. **36**. 1906.

1313-16
LISTER, JOHN, ed. *Court rolls of the manor of Wakefield, vol. III. 1313 to 1316, and 1286.* Y.A.S., R.S. **57**. 1917. Includes abstract of *compotus* of 1305.

1315-17.
LISTER, JOHN, ed. *Court rolls of the manor of Wakefield, vol. IV. 1315 to 1317.* Y.A.S., R.S. **78**. 1930.

1322-31
WALKER, J.W. *Court rolls of the manor of Wakefield, vol V. 1322-1331.* Y.A.S., R.S. **109**. 1945.

1331-3
WALKER, SUE SHERIDAN, ed. *The court rolls of the manor of Wakefield from October 1331 to September 1333.* Y.A.S., W.C.R.S. **3**. 1983.

1348-50
JEWELL, HELEN M., ed. *The court rolls of the manor of Wakefield from September 1348 to September 1350.* Y.A.S., W.C.R.S. **2**. 1981.

1350-52
HABBERJAM, MOIRA, O'REGAN, MARY, & HALE, BRIAN, eds. *The court rolls of the manor of Wkaefield from October 1350 to September 1352.* Y.A.S., W.C.R.S. **6**. 1987.

1537-9
WEIKEL, ANN, ed. *The court rolls of the manor of Wakefield from 1537 to 1539.* Y.A.S., W.C.R.S. **9**. 1993.

1550-52
WEIKEL, ANN, ed. *The court rolls of the manor of Wakefield from October to September 1552.* Y.A.S., W.C.R.S. **7**. 1989.

1583-5
WEIKEL, ANN, ed. *The court rolls of the manor of Wakefield from October 1583 to September 1585.* Y.A.S., W.C.R.S. **4**. 1984.

1608-9
FRASER, C.M., ed. *The court rolls of the manor of Wakefield for 1608/9.* Y.A.S., W.C.R.S. **11**. 1996.

1639-40
FRASER, C.M., & EMSLEY, KENNETH, eds. *The court rolls of the manor of Wakefield from October 1639 to September 1640.* Y.A.S., W.C.R.S., **1**. 1977.

1651-2
ROBINSON, LILIAN, ed. *The court rolls of the manor of Wakefield from 1651 to 1652.* Y.A.S., W.C.R.S. **8**. 1990.

1664-5
FRASER, CONSTANCE M., & EMSLEY, KENNETH, eds. *The court rolls of the manor of Wakefield from October 1664 to September 1665.* Y.A.S., W.C.R.S. **5**. 1986.

1709
CHARLESWORTH, JOHN, ed. *Wakefield manor book 1709.* Y.A.S., R.S. **101**. 1939. Survey, including a descent of the manor.

1790-92
BRENT, ANDREW, ed. *The court rolls of the manor of Wakefield from 1790 to 1792.* Y.A.S., W.C.R.S. **10**. 1994.

Weeland
See Airedale

Wensleydale
WILLAN, T.S., & CROSSLEY, E.W., eds. *Three seventeenth-century Yorkshire surveys.* Y.A.S., R.S., **104**. 1941. Surveys of the manor of Wensleydale, 1614, and the Lordships of Middleham and Richmond, 1605.

West Scrafton
See Hunmanby

Wetherby

UNWIN, R.W. 'A nineteenth-century estate sale: Wetherby, 1824', *Agricultural history review* **23**, 1975, 116-38. Discussion of the sale of the Duke of Devonshire's estate; includes list of leading landowners in Wetherby, and many names of purchasers.

Wharfedale

'Yorkshire families', *Y.C.M.* **1**, 1891, 33-7, 109-14 & 268-73. Extracts from medieval deeds of Wharfedale and Nidderdale.

Wheatley

JACKSON, CHARLES. 'Notes from deeds relating to estates at Wheatley, Bentley, &c., in the County of York, from a ms. book at Wheatley', *Topographer & Genealogist* **3**, 1858, 513-32.

Whitkirk

KIRK, G.E., ed. 'A rental of the bailiwick of Whitkirk', *T.S.* **33**, 1935, 71-82. 1523, from a copy made in 1654-5.

Whitley

BUCKLEY, MICHAEL. 'Saddleworth records part 4: The Beaumonts of Whitley collection in Huddersfield Public Library', *B.S.H.S.* **11**(2), 1981, 29-36. Deed abstracts, 13-17th c.

Wigglesworth

REA, W.F. 'The rental and accounts of Sir Richard Shireburne, 1571-77', *Historic Society of Lancashire and Cheshire transactions* **110**, 1958, 31-57. General discussion, rather than a transcript. Shireburne's properties were in North Lancashire, and in Wigglesworth, Yorkshire.

Wincobank

HALL, T.W. *Material for the history of Wincobank, Sheffield, 1523 to 1750, gathered from the Wheat collection at the Public Reference Library, Sheffield, with abstracts of wills proved at York, relating thereto, and genealogies of the ancient family of Greaves of the parishes of Penistone, Ecclesfield and Sheffield.* Sheffield: J.W. Northend, 1922.

Woodsome Hall

LAW, EDWARD J. 'Woodsome Hall: some estate correspondance', *O.W.R.* **9**, 1989, 26-30. 18th c.

Worsborough

HALL, THOMAS WALTER. *Worsborough, Eckington and Sheffield. Descriptive catalogue of the Edmunds collection, including charters, court-rolls, and extracts relating to Worsborough, Stainborough & Barnsley, near Sheffield; court roll & parliamentary survey of the manor of Eckington, near Sheffield; deeds and wills relating to Sheffield.* Sheffield: J.W. Northend, 1924.

Yeadon

PRICE, G.R., ed. *A transcript of the court rolls of Yeadon, 1361-1476, with the early rentals and accounts of Esholt Priory, charters, deeds and associated material to 1500 A.D., dissolution rentals and accounts.* Draughton: Maple-Bowes Publishers, 1984.

York

LYTE, H.C.MAXWELL. 'The manuscripts of Capt. Josceline F. Bagot', in HISTORICAL MANUSCRIPTS COMMISSION. *Tenth report, Appendix, Part IV.* H.M.S.O., 1885, 318-47. Includes medieval deeds relating to the Hospital of St.Peter at York.

DICKENS, A.G. 'A municipal dissolution of chantries at York, 1536', *Y.A.J.* **36**, 1944-7, 164-73. Includes transcripts of documents naming tenants *etc.*, of York chantry lands.

TRINGHAM, NIGEL J., ed. *Charters of the Vicars Choral of York Minster: City of York and its suburbs to 1546.* Y.A.S., R.S. **148**. 1993.

HODGSON, JOHN. 'Entail in the family of Barton of Fryton, of property in Havergate, York', *Collectanea topographica et genealogica* **2**, 1835, 67-8. 14th c. deed.

WHITE, EILEEN. 'The tenements at the Common Hall Gates, 1550-1725', *York historian* **6**, 1985, 32-42. In York; includes list of tenants.

I. Manorial and other Descents, etc.

Many works on estates are concerned with the owners of particular properties, rather than the properties themselves and their archives. Such works frequently include detailed pedigrees of landowners, or other useful genealogical information. They are listed here by place, but two general works deserve notice first:

WHEATER, W. *Some historic mansions of Yorkshire and their associations.* Leeds: Richard Jackson, 1889. Gives descents.

WOOD, G. BERNARD. *Historic homes of Yorkshire.* Edinburgh: Oliver and Boyd, 1957. Includes notes on some owners.

Acomb Grange
KANER, JENNIFER. 'Acomb Grange', *York historian* 10, 1991, 2-17. Includes descent.

Aske Hall
HARRIS, JOHN. 'The Dundas Empire', *Apollo* 86, 1967, 170-79. Architectural description of Aske Hall, with notes on its descent.

Barkisland
Cliffe
PRIESTLEY, J.H. 'Early settlements', *T. Hal. A.S.* 1943, 97-106. Notes on descent of Cliffe in Barkisland, and Godley in Rishworth.

Lightcliffe Royd
GLEDHILL, HILDA M. 'Lightcliffe Royd, Barkisland', *T. Hal. A.S.* 1969, 1-5. 17-19th c.

Little Even
PRIESTLEY, J.H. 'Little Even', *T. Hal. A.S.* 1940, 47-65. In Barkisland, 15-19th c.

Beauchief Abbey
POTTER, G.R. 'Beauchief Abbey after the dissolution of the monasteries', *T. Hunter A. S.* 11, 1981, 46-50. Notes on descent, 16-20th c.

Birdsall. Vesey Pasture
HAYFIELD, COLIN. 'Vesey Pasture: the development of a Yorkshire Wold Farmstead', *Y.A.J.* 70, 1998, 109-23. At Birdsall; includes information on owners and tenants, 18-20th c.

Birstall
LANCASTER, W.T. 'Birstall, Gomersall and Heckmondwicke', in *Miscellanea* [8]. *T.S.* 26, 1924, 15-40. Descent.

Bolling Hall
SHEERAN, GEORGE. 'Three medieval gentry houses: Bolling Hall, East Riddlesden Hall, and Farnhill Hall', *O.W.R.* 5(2), 1985, 14-19. Includes notes on descents.

Bradford. Brunswick Hall
THACKRAY, CATHERINE. 'Brunswick Place, Bradford: a study based on the census 1841 to 1881', *B.A.* 3rd series 2, 1986, 1-13.

Brighouse
CLAY, H.T. 'Manor of Brighouse notes: from old book 1690-1733', *T. Hal. A.S.* 1943, 107-20.

Bongate Hall
CLAY, H. TRAVIS. 'Bongate Hall, Brighouse', *T. Hal. A.S.* 1938, 281-99. 17-19th c., includes notes on pedigrees of Brighouse, Gill and Ledgard families.

Brigroyd
PRIESTLEY, J.H. 'Brigroyd', *T. Hal. A.S.* 1945, 1-16, 14-16th c.

Broughton Hall
TEMPEST, ELEANOR BLANCHE. 'Broughton Hall and its associations', *B.A.* 6; N.S., 4, 1921, 83-112 & 151-78. 12-19th c.

Burmantofts. Old Hall
LUMB, G.D. 'The Old Hall, Burmantofts', in *Miscellanea* [8]. *T.S.* 26, 1924, 106-12. Descent, 18th c.

Burton Agnes
IMRIE, MARGARET. *The manor houses of Burton Agnes and their owners.* Beverley: Hutton Press, 1993. Includes pedigree of Griffith and Boynton, *etc.,* medieval-20th c.

Carr House
METCALFE, CYRIL. 'Carr House Farm and its documents', *B.A.* 3rd series 4, 1989, 44-52. Descent.

Chellow

ROBERTSHAW, WILFRED. 'The manor of Chellow', *B.A.* **9**; N.S., **7**, 1952, 1-31. Descent; includes folded pedigree of Bolling of Chellow and Ilkley, 15-19th c.

Clayton

ROBERTSHAW, WILFRED. 'The manor of Clayton', *B.A.* **8**; N.S. **6**, 1940, 384-79. Descent, includes folded pedigree of Bolling, 12-15th c.

Lidget

HOLGATE, IVY. 'Lidget in Clayton', *B.A.* **10**; N.S. **8**, 1962, 31-8. Notes on descent, 17th c.

Colden. Great House

KENDALL, HUGH P. 'Great House, in Colden', *P.R.H.A.S.* 1919, 29-48. Descent through Greenwood and Sutcliffe, 16-19th c.

Conisbrough

MACQUIBAN, T.S.A. 'Notes on the history of the Lordship of Conisbrough', *Don. Anc.* 2(2), 1983, 37-9. Includes list of lords, 1561-1935.

Dalton. Dives House

EASTWOOD, DAVID. 'Dives House, Dalton', *O.W.R.* 4(1), 1984, 23-5. See also 4(2), 1984, 33. Descent, 14-20th c.

Danby

SLADE, J.J. 'The Yorkshire estates of the Danvers of Dauntsey', *Wiltshire archaeological and natural history magazine* **50**, 1944, 214-8. Descent of the manor of Danby in the Danvers family, 17th c.

Darfield. New Hall

BIRCH, J. & RYDER, P.F. 'New Hall, Darfield', *Y.A.J.* **54**, 1982, 81-98. Includes descent, medieval-20th c.

Darnall

WALTON, MARY. 'The three Darnall halls', *T. Hunter A.S.* **5**, 1943, 126-30. Notes on descents.

Dobcross. Bridge House

WRIGHT, DANNIE. 'The people of Bridge House', *B.S.H.S.* 24(3), 1994, 16-18. At Dobcross, extracts from parish and nonconformist registers.

East Riddlesden

BRIGG, W.A. 'East Riddlesden Hall and its owners', *B.A.* **2**, 1895, 88-95. Descent. *See also* Bolling Hall

Eccleshill

PRESTON, W.E. 'Notes on the early history of the manor of Eccleshill', *B.A.* **7**; N.S., **5**, 1933, 143-59; **8**; N.S., **6**, 1940, 181-201; **9**; N.S. **7**, 1952, 61-99. Includes pedigrees of Sheffield, 14-15th c., Stanhope, 16-19th c., and Hird of Yeadon, 18th c.

Elland
New Hall

GILES, COLUM. 'New Hall, Elland: the story of a Pennine gentry house from c.1490 to the mid-19th century', *O.W.R.* 1(2), 1981, 1-11. Includes notes on descent, and probate inventory of George Power, 1701.

Lambert House

LONGBOTHAM, A.T. 'Lambert House, Elland', *T. Hal. A.S.* 1933, 45-70. 17-19th c.

Erringden

SENIOR, A. 'Bell House Farm and Erringden Park', *T. Hal. A.S.* 1952, 23-41. At Erringden; notes on descent, 14-19th c.

Exley

ROBERTSHAW, WILFRED. 'The manor and manor house of Exley', *B.A.* **9**; N.S. **7**, 1952, 113-34. Descent; includes folded pedigree of Clapham, 16-17th c.

Farnhill Hall
See Bolling Hall

Gilling Castle

BILSON, JOHN. 'Gilling Castle', *Y.A.J.* **19**, 1906-7, 105-77. Includes pedigrees of Etton and Fairfax, medieval-17th c., extensive list of arms on the stained glass in the living-room; *inquisitions post mortem*, wills, *etc.*

Godley

LISTER, JOHN. 'Early owners of Godley', *P.R.H.A.S.* 1906, 83-103. Medieval-18th c.

Gomersal
See Birstall

Greetland. Clay House

HUNTER, JOSEPH. 'Antiquarian notices of Clay House, in Greteland, in the parish of Halifax and County of York', *Y.A.J.* **2**, 1873, 129-70. Includes descent, especially Clay and Ramsden.

Grimthorpe

DAVIES, ROBERT. 'Grimthorpe: a monograph ...', *Y.A.J.* **2**, 1873, 195-214. Descent.

Halifax

KENDALL, H.P. 'Rectorial manor of Halifax and Heptonstall court rolls', *T. Hal. A.S.* **1937**, 49-153. Late 16th c.

HANSON, T.W. 'Some Halifax houses', *P.R.H.A.S.* 1923, 1-20. Notes on the descents of Parkinson House, Greece House, and Red Hall.

Akeds Road

BRETTON, ROWLAND. 'No. 1, Aked's Road', *T. Hal. A.S.* 1969, 71-4. In Halifax; 19-20th c.

Bentley Royd

'Bentley Royd', *P.R.H.A.S.* 1906, 115-23. Descent, 15-19th c.

Cheapside. Rose and Crown

HARWOOD, H.W. 'The Rose and Crown, Cheapside', *T. Hal. A.S.* 1965, 1-10. 17-20th c.

Clare Hall

WEBSTER, C.D. 'Clare Hall, Halifax', *T. Hal. A.S.* 1967, 123-37. 15-20th c.

Gibraltar Farm

BRETTON, ROWLAND. 'Gibralter Farm', *T. Hal. A.S.* 1983, 77-89. 18-20th c.

Goat House

PRIESTLEY, J.H. 'Goat House and Okes', *T. Hal. A.S.* 1952, 79-86. 16-19th c.

Hope Hall

HANSON, T.W. 'Some old Halifax houses', *P.R.H.A.S.* 1924, 49-64. Notes on Hope Hall and other houses.

PORRITT, A. 'Hope Hall, Halifax, and its past residents', *T. Hal. A.S.* 1972, 77-87. 18-19th c.

Horse Mill

KENDALL, H.P. 'The Horse Mill at Halifax', *T. Hal. A.S.* 1936, 85-92. 16-18th c.

Northgate House

WILSON, JOHN. 'Northgate House, Halifax', *T. Hal. A.S.* 1959, 1-8. 18-19th c.

Stannary End

DENT, G. 'Stannary End, formerly Tymeley Bent', *T. Hal. A.S.* 1929, 273-83. Descent, 17-19th c.

Wood Lane Hall

'Wood Lane Hall', *P.R.H.A.S.* 1906, 124-34. At Halifax; descent, 15-18th c.

Harewood

PARKER, JOHN. 'Some notes on the Lords of Harewood Castle', *Y.A.J.* **22**, 1913, 150-8. Medieval.

MAUCHLINE, MARY. *Harewood House: one of the treasure houses of Britain.* 2nd ed. Ashbourne: Moorland Publishing, 1994. Includes pedigree of Lascelles, 17-20th c.

Hatfield

BIRCH, JULIAN, & RYDER, PETER. 'Hatfield Manor House, South Yorkshire', *Y.A.J.* **60**, 1988, 65-104. Includes descent, medieval-20th c.

Hawksworth Hall

SPEIGHT, HARRY. 'Hawksworth Hall and its associations', *B.A.* N.S. **1**, 1905, 246-92; **2**, 1905, 246-96. Includes notes on descent, medieval-19th c.

Heath. Old Hall

GREEN, LADY. *The Old Hall at Heath, 1568-1888.* Wakefield: W.H.Milnes, 1889. Includes chapters on the families of Kaye, Bolles, Dalston and Smyth, *etc.*

WEAVER, O.J. 'Heath Old Hall, Yorkshire', in APTED, M.R., GILYARD-BEER, R., & SAUNDERS, A.D., eds. *Ancient monuments and their interpretation: essays presented to A. J. Taylor.* Phuillimore, 1977, 285-299. Includes note on descent, 16-20th c., especially on the Kay family.

Hebden Bridge
Birchcliffe Water
GLEDHILL, BARBER. 'Birchcliffe Water, Hebden Bridge', *T. Hal. A.S.* 1962, 35-44. 18th c.

Kings Farm
GLEDHILL, BARBER. 'Kings Farm, or, the White Lion at Hebden Bridge', *T. Hal. A.S.* 1956, 73-92. 17-18th c.

Heckmondwike
See Birdsall

Helmsley Castle
I'ANSON, WILLIAM M. 'Helmsley Castle', *Y.A.J.* **24**, 1906-7, 325-68. Includes brief descent.

Heptonstall
KENDALL, HUGH P. 'Greenwood Lea, Heptonstall', *P.R.H.A.S.* 1917, 113-56. Descent, Medieval-19th c.
See also Halifax

High Sunderland
EMPSALL, T.T. 'High Sunderland, near Halifax', *B.A.* **2**, 1895, 221-8. Includes descent, with notes on the Sunderland family.

Hipperholme. Coley Hall
BRETTON, ROWLAND. 'Coley Hall', *T. Hal. A.S.* 1969, 99-107. In Hipperholme; medieval-20th c.

Holderness
PLANCHE, J.R. 'The early lords of Holderness', *Journal of the British Archaeological Association* **30**, 1874, 121-9.

Holdsworth House
TRIGG, W.B. 'Holdsworth House', *T. Hal. A.S.* 1942, 29-44. 15-18th c.

Horton
KING, J.S. 'The manor of Horton in Bradford-Dale', *B.A.* **11**; N.S. **9**, 1976, 210-14. 17-19th c.

Hove Edge. Netherhouse
BRETTON, ROWLAND. 'Netherhouse, Hove Edge', *T. Hal. A.S.* 1965, 11-21. 17-20th c.

Howley
BAILDON, W. PALEY. 'The early history of Howley', *Y.N.Q.I.* **2**, 1890, 105-21. Descent through Rotherfield, Mirfield and Wentworth, medieval-16th c.

Hull. Salthouse Lane
GODDEN, ANN. 'The house on Salthouse Lane', in CROWTHER, JAN, & CROWTHER, PETER, eds. *Collected articles from the Bulletin of the East Yorkshire Local History Society bulletin, nos 1-55, 1970-Feb 1997.* [ ]: the Society, 1997, vol. I, 95-8. Originally published in the *Bulletin* **53**, 1995/6, 17-21. Descent of a Hull property, 18-20th c.

Ilkley
See Chellow

Illingworth
Maude House
TRIGG, W.B. 'Maude House, Illingworth', *T. Hal. A.S.* 1945, 17-28. 16-19th c.

Ryecroft
TRIGG, W.B. 'Ryecroft, Illingworth', *T. Hal. A.S.* 1929, 209-48. Descent, 16-19th c.

Jordans
'The Jordans', *R. & D.F.H.S.N.* **2**, 1984, unpaginated (9 pp.) Includes list of occupants, 19-20th c.
BERRY, A.R. 'The Jordans', *F.S.* **12**(1), 1991, 25-6; **12**(2), 1991, 47-9. Reprinted from *R. & D.F.H.S.J.* Descent, 18-20th c.

Keighley
WHONE, CLIFFORD. 'A mill and two carucates in Keighley', *B.A.* **9**; N.S., **7**, 1952, 135-60. Descent.

Kilton
HEBDITCH, W. 'The origin and early history of the Kilton fee', *Y.A.J.* **34**, 1939, 269-309.

Kirby Wiske
B[RUCE], W.D. 'Some notice of the descent of the principal estates in the parish of Kirby-Wiske, in the North Riding of Yorkshire', *Topographer & genealogist* **1**, 1846, 294-9.

Kirkby Malzeard

GOWLAND, TOM S. 'The Honour of Kirkby Malzeard and the Chase of Nidderdale', *Y.A.J.* **33**, 1938, 349-96.

Langfield. Stoodley

NEWELL, ABRAHAM. 'Stoodley in Langfield and its associations', *P.R.H.A.S.* 1918, 69-99. With the Stodeley, Horsfall and Knowles families, medieval-19th c.

Leeds. Briggate

LUMB, G.D. 'The last shop with bow windows in Briggate, Leeds', in *Miscellanea* **[8]**. *T.S.* **26**, 1924, 397-403. Descent, 17-19th c.

Lightcliffe. Giles House

BRETTON, R. 'Giles House, Lightcliffe', *T. Hal. A.S.* 1943, 87-94, 16-19th c.

Littleborough. Pyke House

TRIGG, W.B. 'Pyke House, Littleborough', *T. Hal. A.S.* 1933, 71-77. 17-19th c.

Lower Siddall Hall

BRETTON, R. 'Lower Siddall Hall', *T. Hal. A.S.* 1960, 77-83. 16-19th c.

Lower Warley

SUTCLIFFE, TOM. 'A tour through Lower Warley', *P.R.H.A.S.* 1926, 101-22. Includes notes on house descents.

Luddenden
Old Riding

SENIOR, A. 'Old Riding, Luddenden', *T. Hal. A.S.* 1949, 1-12. Medieval-19th c.

Peel House Mills

HARWOOD, H.W. 'Peel House Mills', *T. Hal. A.S.* 1946, 51-9. At Luddenden; 18-19th c.

Manningham. Godbrigg

PRESTON, WILLIAM E. 'Godbrigg in Manningham', *B.A.* **10**; N.S. **8**, 1962, 21-30. Notes on 16th c. descent.

Middlesbrough

PATTENDEN, D.W. 'Joseph Pease and the owners of the Middlesbrough estate', *C.T.L.H.S.B.* **41**, 1981, 26-31. Includes pedigree showing inter-relationship of Birkbeck, Pease, Richardson and Whitwell, 18-20th c.

Midgley

SUTCLIFFE, TOM. 'A tour in Midgley', *P.R.H.A.S.* 1927, 113-57. Notes on house descents.

HARWOOD, H.W. 'Four Midgley farms,' *T. Hal. A.S.* 1939, 213-63. Notes on descents.

Brearley Halls

SUTCLIFFE, TOM. 'The Brearley Halls in Midgley', *P.R.H.A.S.* 1922, 125-60. Descent, 15-19th c., includes will of Hugh Lacye, 1573.

Castle Carr

SUTCLIFFE, TOM. 'Castle Carr in Midgley', *P.R.H.A.S.* 1921, 97-108. Includes notes on descent, mainly 19th c.

Dean House

HARWOOD, H.W. 'Dean House, Midgley', *T. Hal. A.S.* 1960, 1-11. Medieval-19th c.

Ewood

DENT, G. 'Ewood in Midgley', *T. Hal. A.S.* 1939, 7-70. 14-18th c.

Great House

HARWOOD, H.W. 'Great House, Midgley', *T. Hal. A.S.* 1954, 69-76. 17-20th c.

Hauroyd

HARWOOD, H.W. 'Hauroyd in Midgley', *T. Hal. A.S.* 1955, 77-85. 16-19th c.

Manor Mill

HARWOOD, H.W. 'Midgley's Manor Mill', *T. Hal. A.S.* 1958, 51-62. Medieval-19th c.

Oats Royd

SUTCLIFFE, TOM. 'Oats Royd in Midgley', *P.R.H.A.S.* 1920, 63-82. Descent through Farrar, Lacy and Murgatroyd, 16-19th c.

Mirfield. Blake Hall

NUSSEY, JOHN. 'Blake Hall, in Mirfield, and its occupants during the 18th and 19th centuries', *Y.A.J.* **5**, 1983, 119-141. Descent, especially Turner and Ingham families.

Mixenden. Clough

TRIGG, W.B. 'Clough in Mixenden', *T. Hal. A.S.* 1942, 19-26. 16-18th c.

Nidderdale
See Kirkby Malzeard

Norland
KENDALL, H.P. 'Ancient halls of Norland', *P.R.H.A.S.* 1904-5, 93-111. Descents.

Lower Wat Ing
WILSON, JOHN. 'Lower Wat Ing, in Norland', *T. Hal. A.S.* 1957, 11-14. 18-19th c.

Northowram
HANSON, T.W. 'Two Northowram homesteads', *B.A.* 11; N.S., 9, 1976, 86-103. Notes on descent.

Marsh Hall
BRETTON, R. 'Marsh Hall, Northowram', *T. Hal. A.S.* 1958, 91-5. Medieval-19th c.

Northowram Hall
TRIGG, W.B. 'Northowram Hall', *T. Hal. A.S.* 1932, 129-52. Descent, 13-19th c.

Ovenden
TRIGG, W.B. 'Some Ovenden houses', *P.R.H.A.S.* 1928, 321-75. Notes on house descents.
WILSON, JOHN. 'Notes on some Ovenden houses', *T. Hal. A.S.* 1961, 37-54. Notes on the descent of various houses.

Sod House Green
TRIGG, T.W. 'Sod House Green', *P.R.H.A.S.* 1927, 129-38. In Ovenden; descent, 18-19th c.

Pudsey. Nesbit Hall
STRONG, RUTH. 'Nesbit Hall: the old Bank House', *Y.A.J.* 70, 1998, 101-8. At Pudsey; descent, 16-20th c.

Rastrick
CLAY, H.TRAVIS. 'Some Rastrick houses', *T. Hal. A.S.* 1935, 141-73. Many notes on descents; includes folded pedigree of Hanson of Rastrick Hall, 16-17th c.

Ripon
GOWLAND, TOM. S. 'The manors and liberties of Ripon', *Y.A.J.* 32, 1936, 43-85.

Market Place
DENTON, JEAN. 'Ripon Market Place research project (1). The Wakeman's House', *R.H.* 1(6), 1991, 1-5. See also 3(2), 1996, 45. Descent, 17-19th c.
PLACE, A.H. 'No. 6, Market Place, Ripon', *R.H.* 2(1), 1993, 17-21. Descent, 17-20th c., includes pedigree of Oxley.
DENTON, JEAN. 'Ripon Market Place research. Barclays Bank, no. 7', *R.H.* 2(10), 1995, 242-6. Descent, 17-20th c.
DENTON, JEAN. '8 and 9, Market Place, Ripon', *R.H.* 2(11), 1995, 270-73. Descent, 17-20th c.
PLACE, A.H. '11 and 12, Market Place, Ripon (now Dorothy Perkins)', *R.H.* 3(5), 1997, 128-30. Descent, 14-20th c.
DENTON, JEAN. 'Ripon Market Place research (10): no. 19', *R.H.* 11(6), 1994, 134-6. Descent, 17-20th c.
DENTON, JEAN. '20/21, Market Place, Ripon', *R.H.* 2(7), 1994, 166-9. Descent, 17-20th c.
PLACE, ANTHONY. '25/26, Market Place, Ripon', *R.H.* 3(6), 1997, 151-4. Descent, 17-20th c.
DENTON, JEAN. '28/29, Market Place, Ripon (Burtons)', *R.H.* 2(9), 1995, 213-6. Descent, 17-20th c.
DENTON, JEAN. 'Ripon Market Place research (12). Nos. 30,31 and 31A', *R.H.* 2(8), 1994, 189-93. Descent, 16-20th c.
DENTON, JEAN. 'Ripon, Market Place research (4): no. 34. Becket's House', *R.H.* 1(9), 1992, 7-9. Descent, 17-20th c.
DENTON, JEAN. 'Ripon Market Place research: (4): the Yorkshire Bank', *R.H.* 1(10), 1992, 6-10. Descent of 35-6, Market Place, 17-20th c.
WHITEHEAD, J.K. 'Ripon Market Place research. No. 38: the Town Hall', *R.H.* 2(12), 1995, 309-11; 3(1), 1996, 18-25; 3(2), 1996, 46-9; 3(4), 1996, 103-7. Descent, 17-20th c.
HAYWARD, GEOFF. 'Numbers 39 & 40, Market Place, Ripon', *R.H.* 2(3), 1993, 52-4. Descent, 17-20th c.
DENTON, JEAN. 'Ripon Market Place research: house number 41', *R.H.* 2(2), 1993, 38-40. Descent, 18-20th c.
SHERWOOD, DOROTHY. '42, Market Place, Ripon', *R.H.* 2(5), 1994, 111-14. Descent, 17-20th c.

Ripponden
The Height
PRIESTLEY, JOHN H. 'Old Ripponden: the Height and the Chappel', *T. Hal. A.S.* 1932, 185-202. 15-19th c.

Ripponden Wood
PRIESTLEY, J.H. 'Ripponden Wood', *T. Hal. A.S.* 1946, 27-34. Notes on the descent of various properties *etc.*

Rishworth
Booth
PRIESTLEY, J.H. 'Booth and Wormald, Rishworth', *T. Hal. A.S.* 1938, 197-228. 14-17th c.

Godley
See Barkisland

Romanby
A., G.J. 'Descent of some of the principal property in Romanby township, in the parish of North Allerton, North Riding of Yorkshire', *Topographer & genealogist* **1**, 1846, 323-9. See also 496.

Rooley Hall
PRESTON, WM. E. 'Rooley Hall and its associations', *B.A.* **7**; N.S., **5**, 1933, 33-49. 16-18th c.

Royds Hall
BRETTON, R. 'Royds Hall', *T. Hal. A.S.* 1936, 165-91. 16-19th c.

Scout Hall
TRIGG, W.B., 'Scout Hall', *T. Hal. A.S.* 1946, 37-47. 15-20th c.

Sheffield
TUCKER, STEPHEN T. 'Descent of the manor of Sheffield', *Journal of the British Archaeological Association* **30**, 1874, 237-77. See also 489-93 for index. Includes poll taxes for 1379 and 1692, hearth tax 1665, and list of smiths and cutlers, 1670.
LEADER, R.E. 'The house at the Church Gates', *T. Hunter A.S.* **1**(1), 1914, 71-80; **1**(2), 1917, 173-86. Descent of a Sheffield house, 16-19th c.

Shibden
PEARSON, MARK. 'Ancient Shibden mansions', *P.R.H.A.S.* 1906, 141-64. Descents of Staups, Field House, Salterlea, and Damhead.

Dore House
LISTER, J. 'The history of Dore House, now the Shibden Industrial School', *P.R.H.A.S.* 1924, 127-68. Medieval.

Shibden Hall
LISTER, J. 'The history of Shibden Hall', *P.R.H.A.S.* 1915, 149-52; 1916, 261-92; 1917, 53-88; 1921, 129-68; 1923, 101-22; 1925, 57-78; 1926, 1-11; 1935; 41-59.
LISTER, JOHN. 'History of Shibden Hall in the early eighteenth century', *T. Hal. A.S.* 1936, 1-25.

Shirecliffe Hall
WALTON, MARY. 'Shirecliffe Hall', *T. Hunter A.S.* **5**, 1943, 53-60. Includes descent, 16-19th c.

Skircoat
KENDALL, H.P. 'Some old Skircoat homestead', *P.R.H.A.S.* 1925, 1-36. Notes on various house descents.

Heath Hall
BRETTON, ROWLAND. 'Heath Hall, Skircoat', *T. Hal. A.S.* 1968, 1-14. 18-19th c.

Wood Hall
BRETTON, R. 'Wood Hall, Skircoat', *T. Hal. A.S.* 1955, 19-32. 16-20th c.

Slead Hall
CLAY, H. TRAVIS. 'Slead Hall', *T. Hal. A.S.* 1993, 169-93. 16-18th c.

Southowram
Ashday
BRETTON, R. 'Ashday in Southowram', *T. Hal. A.S.* 1942, 75-94. 13-20th c.

Ash Grove
LAW, EDWARD J. 'Ash Grove, Southowram', *O.W.R.* **8**(1), 1988, 8-10. Descent, 19-20th c.

Marsh Farm
LEE, W.J. 'Marsh Farm, Southowram', *T. Hal. A.S.* 1952, 71-8. 17-19th c.

Sowerby

Asquithbottom
KENDALL, H.P. 'Asquithbottom or Old House',
T. Hal. A.S. 1935, 55-68. In Sowerby
Bridge; descent 16-18th c.

Lower Deerplay
CROSSLEY, E.W. 'Lower Deerplay', *P.R.H.A.S.*
1907, 139-57. In Sowerby; descent,
15-18th c.

Sowerby Mill
KENDALL, H.P. 'The Mill at the Brigg',
P.R.H.A.S. 1923, 159-88. Sowerby Mill,
16-20th c.

White Windows
KENDALL, H.P. 'Famous Sowerby mansion:
White Windows', *P.R.H.A.S.* 1906, 105-15.
Descent, 16-19th c.

Soyland

Blackshaw Clough
KENDALL, HUGH P. 'Blackshaw Clough, in
Soyland', *P.R.H.A.S.* 1916, 133-41. Descent,
16-17th c.

Making Place
KENDALL, HUGH P. 'Making Place, in
Soyland, and the Hill family', *P.R.H.A.S.*
1916, 9-70. Descent.

Smallees
PRIESTLEY, J.H. 'Smallees in Soyland', *T. Hal.
A.S.* 1957, 37-9. 16-18th c.

The Lumb
KENDALL, HUGH P. 'The Lumb in Soyland',
T. Hal. A.S. 1933, 1-23. 14-19th c.

The Royd
KENDALL, HUGH P. 'The Royd, in Soyland',
P.R.H.A.S. 1916, 113-30. Descent; includes
folded pedigree of Royde, 16-18th c.

Stott Hill Hall
ROBERTSHAW, WILFRID. 'Stott Hill Hall
and its associations', *B.A.* 7; N.S., 5,
1933, 193-215. Includes folded pedigree
of Priestley, of Shelf and Bradford,
18-19th c., also of Skelton, of Pickering
and Bradford, 18th c.

Tong
ROBERTSHAW, WILFRID. 'The manor of Tong',
B.A. 10; N.S., 8, 1962, 69-89 & 117-29. Pt. 1.
The family of Tong, lords of Tong. Pt. 2.
The family of Mirfield, lords of Tong.

Tyersall
ROBERTSHAW, WILFRID. 'The hamlet or
manor of Tyersall', *B.A.* 9; N.S. 7, 1952,
161-89. Descent, includes folded pedigree
of Thornton, 15-18th c.

Wadsworth

Birchenlee Carr
DENT, G. 'Birchenlee Carr, or Birckenlee
Carr', *T. Hal. A.S.* 1931, 133-72. In
Wadsworth; descent, medieval-19th c.

Redacarr
DENT, G. 'Redacre, Redicarre in Wadsworth',
T. Hal. A.S. 1930, 65-76. Descent,
medieval-17th c.

Wadsworth Royd
DENT, G. 'Wadsworth Royd in Wadsworth',
T. Hal. A.S. 1933, 25-42. 16-19th c.

Wainstalls

Lower Slack
HARWOOD, H.W. 'Lower Slack, Wainstalls',
T. Hal. A.S. 1952, 115-22. 17-19th c.

Wainstalls Mills
HARWOOD, H.W. 'Wainstalls Mills', *T. Hal.
A.S.* 1954, 65-8. 19th c.

Walkley Hall
'Walkley Hall', *T. Hunter A.S.* 3, 1929, 165-
71. Descent, 17-18th c.

Warley

Cawsey
KENDALL, H.P. 'Cawsey in Warley', *T. Hal.
A.S.* 1936, 69-82. 16-18th c.

Cliff Hill
SUTCLIFFE, TOM. 'Cliff Hill, in Warley',
P.R.H.A.S. 1917, 205-63. Descent; includes
pedigree of Milne, undated.

Hartley Royd
HARWOOD, H.W. 'Hartley Royd, Warley',
T. Hal. A.S. 1966, 19-25. Medieval-20th c.

Hollins

SUTCLIFFE, TOM. 'The Hollins in Warley and its families', *P.R.H.A.S.* 1915, 281-323. Descent; includes folded pedigree of Dearden, 17-19th c.

Peel House

SUTCLIFFE, TOM. 'Peel House in Warley', *P.R.H.A.S.* 1920, 53-62. Descent through Wade, Smith Hamerton, and Ambler, 16-19th c.

Saltonstall

SUTCLIFFE, TOM. 'Saltonstall in Warley', *P.R.H.A.S.* 1921, 109-128. Descent; includes folded pedigree of Saltonstall, 14-17th c.

The Bache

KENDALL, H.P. 'The Bache in Warley', *P.R.H.A.S.* 1927, 45-75.

The Hill

HANSON, T.W. 'The Hill, Warley', *T. Hal. A.S.* 1942, 63-70. 16-19th c.

The Stepps

KENDALL, H.P. 'The Stepps in Warley', *T. Hal. A.S.* 1932, 69-92. Descent, medieval-18th c., with pedigree of Crowther, 14-17th c.

Welton Hall

EVANS, NICHOLAS. 'A history of Welton Hall', *B.T.* **60**, 1994, 16-17. Descent, 18-20th c.

Wetherby

BRETT, ALFRED. 'The manor of Wetherby, and lands within the manor', *Y.A.J.* **30**, 1931, 261-73. Descent.

Wheatley. City Fold.

TRIGG, W.B., & DENT, G. 'City Fold, Wheatley', *T. Hal. A.S.* 1934, 155-88. 16-19th c.

Wilsden

FAWCETT, R.H. 'The story of Wilsden', *B.A.* **11**; N.S. **9**, 1976, 1-28, 131-50 & 187-209.

Wressle Castle

'Wressle Castle', *Y.A.J.* **22**, 1913, 182-93. Includes notes on its descent and heraldry.

York

Fairfax House

BROWN, PETER. *Fairfax House, York: an illustrated history and guide.* York: York Civic Trust, 1989. Includes chapter on 'the owners'.

Treasurers House

FORRESTER, RICHARD. 'Owners and occupiers of Treasurers House, York, 1815-1900', *York historian* **10**, 1992, 52-63.

GRAY, EDWIN, MRS. *The Mansion House of the Treasurers of York Minster, now Treasurers House and Grays Court.* York: Ben Jonson & Co., 1933. Provides much information on owners since 1547.

Author Index

82

Family Name Index

Place Name Index

86

90